Strategic READING 1
Building Effective Reading Skills

Student's Book

CAMBRIDGE
UNIVERSITY PRESS

Jack C. Richards   Samuela Eckstut-Didier

PUBLISHED BY THE PRESS SYNDICATE OF THE UNIVERSITY OF CAMBRIDGE
The Pitt Building, Trumpington Street, Cambridge, United Kingdom

CAMBRIDGE UNIVERSITY PRESS
The Edinburgh Building, Cambridge CB2 2RU, UK
40 West 20th Street, New York, NY 10011–4211, USA
10 Stamford Road, Oakleigh, VIC 3166, Australia
Ruiz de Alarcón 13, 28014 Madrid, Spain
Dock House, The Waterfront, Cape Town 8001, South Africa

http://www.cambridge.org

First published 2003

Printed in the United States of America

Typeface Baskerville Book   *System* QuarkXPress®   [AH]

A catalog record for this book is available from the British Library

Library of Congress Cataloging in Publication data available

ISBN 0 521 555809   Student's Book 1
ISBN 0 521 555779   Teacher's Manual 1
ISBN 0 521 555795   Student's Book 2
ISBN 0 521 555760   Teacher's Manual 2
ISBN 0 521 555787   Student's Book 3
ISBN 0 521 555752   Teacher's Manual 3

Art direction, book design, and layout services: Adventure House, NYC

Contents

Authors' Acknowledgments

The publisher would like to thank the following **reviewers** for their helpful insights and suggestions: Orlando Carranza, Ann Conable, Elliot Judd, Madeleine Kim, Laura LeDréan, Laura MacGregor, Sandy Soghikian, Colleen Weldele, and Junko Yamanaka.

We would also like to acknowledge the **students** and **teachers** in the following schools and institutes who piloted materials in the initial development stages:

Associaçao Alumni, São Paulo, Brazil; **American University Alumni**, Bangkok, Thailand; **Case Western Reserve University**, Cleveland, Ohio, USA; **Hokusei Gakuen University**, Sapporo, Japan; **Hunter College**, New York, New York, USA; **Instituto Brasil-Estados Unidos** (**IBEU**), Rio de Janeiro, Brazil; **Instituto Cultural Peruano Norteamericano**, Lima, Peru; **Kyung Hee University**, Seoul, Korea; **Miyagi Gakuin Women's College**, Miyagi, Japan; **Queens College**, Flushing, New York, USA; **Sapporo International University**, Sapporo, Japan.

We also would like to thank the many additional schools in the above countries whose students responded to surveys on their reading interests and preferences.

A special thanks to Lynn Bonesteel and Robert L. Maguire for their invaluable advice and support. The authors are also grateful to Chuck Sandy for his contribution to the early development of the project.

Thanks also go to the **editorial** and **production** team: Eleanor Barnes, Sylvia Bloch, David Bohlke, Karen Davy, Tünde Dewey, Anne Garrett, Deborah Goldblatt, Nada Gordon, Louisa Hellegers, Bill Paulk, Mary Sandre, Howard Siegelman, Jane Sturtevant, and Louisa van Houten.

Finally, special thanks to Cambridge University Press **staff** and **advisors**: Jim Anderson, Mary Louise Baez, Carlos Barbisan, Kathleen Corley, Kate Cory-Wright, Riitta da Costa, Elizabeth Fuzikava, Steve Golden, Yuri Hara, Gareth Knight, Andy Martin, Nigel McQuitty, Mark O'Neil, Dan Schulte, Catherine Shih, Su-Wei Wang, and Ellen Zlotnick.

Scope and sequence

Unit	Readings	Skills	Vocabulary
Unit 1 **Music**	Music & moods Louis Armstrong The biology of music	Distinguishing main and supporting ideas Guessing meaning from context Predicting Recognizing tone Scanning Understanding details Understanding main ideas Understanding text organization	Kinds of music Musical instruments Musical terms Musicians
Unit 2 **Money**	Dangers in shopping How to be a millionaire Pity the poor lottery winner	Guessing meaning from context Predicting Restating Scanning Understanding details Understanding main ideas	Financial terms Terms for spending habits
Unit 3 **Work**	Your first job Job satisfaction Are you a workaholic?	Guessing meaning from context Making inferences Predicting Recognizing audience Restating Scanning Understanding details Understanding main ideas	Job-related terms Work idioms

Unit 4
Sports
	Do pro athletes make too
	   much money?
	
	Extreme sports
	
	Frequently asked questions
	   about the ancient
	   Olympic Games
		Distinguishing arguments
		Guessing meaning from context
		Making inferences
		Predicting
		Scanning
		Understanding details
		Understanding meaning from
		   related forms
		Understanding text organization
			Action verbs
			Names of sports
			Sports equipment
			Sports locales

Unit	Readings	Skills	Vocabulary
Unit 5 **Weather**	Keeping an eye on the weather Nature's weather forecasters Could you survive a natural disaster?	Guessing meaning from context Predicting Scanning Understanding details Understanding main ideas Understanding text organization	Natural disasters Weather conditions Weather measurements Word formation
Unit 6 **Clothes**	Dressing for success Casual dress in the workplace T-shirts out; uniforms in	Distinguishing arguments Guessing meaning from context Interpreting meaning in specific contexts Predicting Scanning Skimming Understanding details Understanding main ideas	Fashion terms Phrasal verbs
Unit 7 **Culture**	Adventures in India Body language in the United States Cross-cultural differences	Guessing meaning from context Making inferences Recognizing audience Scanning Understanding details Understanding main ideas	Adjectives (positive and negative descriptions) Prefixes
Unit 8 **Outer space**	Living in space The planets Space tours not so far off	Guessing meaning from context Making inferences Predicting Scanning Skimming Understanding details Understanding main ideas	Homonyms Space terms

Unit	Readings	Skills	Vocabulary
Unit 9 **Animals**	The terrible toads Exotic animals — not as pets! Let's abandon zoos	Distinguishing fact from opinion Guessing meaning from context Making inferences Predicting Recognizing similarity in meaning Scanning Skimming Understanding main ideas Understanding a sequence of events	Animal idioms Animal names Animal-related terms
Unit 10 **Travel**	Adventure travel Choosing an ecodestination Jet lag	Guessing meaning from context Making inferences Predicting Scanning Skimming Summarizing Understanding details	Vacation activities Vacation places Vacation provisions
Unit 11 **The Internet**	Love on the Internet Help on the Internet Count me out	Guessing meaning from context Making inferences Predicting Recognizing tone Scanning Skimming Understanding details Understanding a sequence of events	Computer terms Phrasal verbs
Unit 12 **Friends**	Ten easy ways to make friends Best friends The new family	Distinguishing main and supporting ideas Guessing meaning from context Making inferences Predicting Scanning Skimming Understanding details Understanding reference words	Adjectives (descriptions of friends and friendships) Word formation

Unit	Readings	Skills	Vocabulary
Unit 13 **Gifts**	Gift giving Modern day self-sacrifice Gifts for the hard to please	Guessing meaning from context Interpreting meaning in specific contexts Predicting Recognizing sources Scanning Understanding details Understanding main ideas Understanding a sequence of events	Gift-related terms Homonyms
Unit 14 **Emotions**	Jokes can't always make you laugh Envy: Is it hurting or helping you? The value of tears	Guessing meaning from context Predicting Recognizing sources Restating and making inferences Scanning Understanding details Understanding main ideas Understanding reference words	Characteristics and traits Feelings Word families
Unit 15 **Food**	Chocolate What our taste buds say about us It tastes just like chicken	Guessing meaning from context Recognizing audience Recognizing point of view Scanning Understanding details Understanding main ideas	Adjectives (descriptions of flavors) Cooking terms Food preferences
Unit 16 **Sleep &** **dreams**	Power napping is good for the I.Q. Common questions about dreams What is a dream?	Guessing meaning from context Predicting Restating and making inferences Scanning Skimming Understanding complex sentences Understanding details Understanding reference words	Sleep advice Sleep habits Sleep terms

Introduction

Overview

Featuring adapted texts from a variety of authentic sources, including newspapers, magazines, books, and websites, the *Strategic Reading* series allows students to build essential reading skills while they examine important topics in their lives.

Strategic Reading 1 is designed to develop the reading, vocabulary-building, and critical thinking skills of young-adult and adult learners of English at a low-intermediate to intermediate level.

Format

Each book in the *Strategic Reading* series contains 16 units divided into three readings on a particular theme. Every unit includes the sections described below:

Preview

The units begin with brief descriptions previewing the readings in the unit. These descriptions are accompanied by discussion questions designed to stimulate student interest and activate background knowledge on the theme.

This page also introduces some of the vocabulary found in the readings. These words and phrases are recycled throughout the unit to provide students with many opportunities to process and internalize new vocabulary.

Readings

Different readings have been gathered from novels, plays, magazines, textbooks, websites, poetry, newspapers, editorials, and personal journals to reflect realistically the varied nature of the written world. These texts increase gradually in length and difficulty as students progress through the book. A full page of challenging exercises, divided into the following three sets of activities, focuses students on each reading.

Before you read

This section encourages students to think more carefully about a specific area of the theme. When students make predictions based on their personal experiences, a valuable link between background knowledge and new information is formed.

Reading

One *Skimming* or *Scanning* activity accompanies every reading in the book. In this section, students must either skim or scan a passage to look for specific information or to confirm predictions made in the pre-reading activity. After, students are instructed to read the whole text.

After you read

The exercises in this section concentrate on the following reading skills (see the Scope and sequence chart on pages vi–ix) developed throughout the book:

- understanding main ideas and details;

- making inferences and guessing meaning from context;

- understanding the organization and cohesion of a text;

- recognizing an audience, source, tone, or point of view;

- distinguishing fact from opinion; and

- understanding complex sentences and the sequence of events.

In order to focus on multiple skills and accommodate different learning and teaching styles, a wide variety of task types are featured in these exercises. These task types include multiple choice, matching, true/false, and fill in the blank. These varied activities are designed to practice all aspects of a particular skill, and to maintain the interest of both students and teachers.

Each reading ends with an exercise called *Relating reading to personal experience* that allows students to use vocabulary introduced in the unit to share their thoughts, opinions, and experiences in writing or in discussions.

Wrap-up

Every unit ends with a one-page review section where students apply and expand their knowledge of unit vocabulary to complete a variety of fun and challenging word games and puzzles.

As a final activity, students work on a project or participate in a discussion related to the unit theme. Activities such as designing and conducting surveys, researching and presenting information, and interviewing others provide meaningful closure to the unit.

Strategic Reading 1 is accompanied by a Teacher's Manual that contains a model lesson plan, definitions of key vocabulary, comprehensive teaching suggestions, cultural notes, unit quizzes, and answers to activities and quizzes.

UNIT 1 | Music

You are going to read three texts about music. First, answer the questions in the boxes.

READING 1

Music & moods

Feeling sad? Why not change your mood with music? This magazine article explains the effect of music on people's emotions.

1. What are your favorite kinds of music?
2. How do different kinds of music make you feel?

READING 2

Louis Armstrong

People around the world love the music of Louis Armstrong. Find out how this brilliant jazz musician got his start.

1. What do you think about jazz?
2. Do you know the music of Louis Armstrong? If so, do you like it?

READING 3

The biology of music

What is music? How is it different from speech? Learn more about the connection between music and the human brain.

1. How do humans communicate through music? What about animals?
2. Can you give an example of how music expresses emotion?

Vocabulary

Look at the CD covers and the words in the boxes. Circle the words you already know. Give examples of the words you circled.

musician   song

Latin music   band

composer   note

Music & moods

1   Have you ever felt a sudden rush of joy because a favorite song came on the radio? Then you know that music can have a strong effect on your emotions. You should try to take advantage of this power of music. It can help you beat a bad mood or maintain a good mood, says Alicia Ann Clair, professor of music therapy at the University of Kansas. Music can also help you relax and feel rejuvenated.

2   To cheer up or boost energy, listen to Latin music or anything with accented beats, lots of percussion, and a fast tempo. When you want to relax after a busy day, music with string instruments and woodwinds, less percussion, and a slower tempo can calm you.

3   Listen to calming music before you tackle stressful activities, recommends Dr. Clair. "Once you're in a good state of mind, it's easier to maintain." To reduce stress at work, put on relaxing tunes only when you really need them. "If you listen to them all day long, you will screen them out," Dr. Clair explains.

4   You can change your mood by switching from one kind of music to another. To feel rejuvenated, "Start with something serene and relaxing, then gradually pick up the tempo and beat," says Dr. Clair. For example, play Frank Sinatra ballads, then move on to something energetic such as Aretha Franklin. When you want to calm down after a busy week at work, do the opposite.

Adapted from *Woman's Day.*

Percussion instruments

Woodwind instruments

String instruments

READING TIP

When you need to find specific information, scan the text. Look through it quickly to find the information without reading every sentence.

Before you read

Check (✔) the statements that are true about you.

_____ 1. To cheer up, I listen to music with lots of percussion and a fast tempo.

_____ 2. When I don't feel very energetic, I listen to Latin music because the accented beats give me more energy.

_____ 3. When I want to relax after a busy day, I listen to music with string and woodwind instruments and a slow tempo.

_____ 4. Before I do something stressful, I listen to calming music.

_____ 5. When I want to change my mood, I first listen to one kind of music. Then I change to another kind of music.

Reading

Scan the text to find the writer's advice. Circle the statements above that the writer agrees with. Then read the whole text.

After you read

A **Write the number of each paragraph next to its main idea.**

_4_ a. This paragraph describes music that can change your mood.

_____ b. This paragraph describes music that affects people's energy level.

_____ c. This paragraph describes why music is important in people's lives.

_____ d. This paragraph describes music that can help people with stress.

B **Find the words in _italics_ in the reading. Circle the meaning of each word.**

1. When you _beat a bad mood_, your bad mood **starts** / **stops.** (par. 1)
2. When you feel _rejuvenated_, you feel more **tired** / **energetic**. (pars. 1 and 4)
3. When you _boost_ energy, you have **more** / **less** energy. (par. 2)
4. When you _tackle_ something, you deal with something **easy** / **difficult**. (par. 3)
5. If you _screen_ music _out_, you **listen** / **do not pay attention** to it. (par. 3)
6. _Serene_ music is **loud and fast** / **peaceful and calm**. (par. 4)
7. A _ballad_ is a **slow love song** / **fast dance song**. (par. 4)

C **Answer these questions.**

1. What music do you listen to when you are in a bad mood? What about when you are in a good mood?
2. What is your favorite musical instrument? Why do you like it?
3. What is a good piece of music to listen to before you do something stressful?

Louis Armstrong

1   Louis Armstrong had two famous nicknames. Some people called him Satchmo, short for "Satchel Mouth." They said his mouth looked like a satchel, or large bag. Musicians were more likely to call him Pops, as a sign of respect for his influence on the world of music.

2   Armstrong was born on August 4, 1901, in Jane Alley, one of the toughest areas of New Orleans, Louisiana. He grew up poor, but surrounded by great musicians. Jazz was invented in New Orleans a few years before he was born. Armstrong often said, "Jazz and I grew up together."

3   Armstrong was arrested in his early teens for a minor offense. That arrest proved to be lucky. He was sent to a boy's home where Professor Peter Davis taught him to play the cornet. Armstrong had a great talent for music, and he went quickly from being the bass drummer in the school band to first bugler and cornetist.

4   On leaving the boys' home in his late teens, Armstrong began to live the life of a musician. He played with bands in parades, clubs, and on the steamboats that traveled on the Mississippi River. At that time, the city was defined by the new music of jazz and was home to many great musicians. Armstrong learned from the older musicians and soon became respected as their equal. He was the best student of the great cornetist and trumpeter Joe Oliver, and played second cornet in his famous band, King Oliver's Creole Jazz Band.

5   In 1918, Joe Oliver moved to Chicago. At first, Armstrong remained in New Orleans, but in 1922 he went to Chicago to rejoin Oliver's band. There, the tale of Louis Armstrong, the genius, begins. From then until the end of his life, Armstrong was celebrated, imitated, and loved wherever he went. Armstrong had no equal when it came to playing the American popular song.

6   His trumpet playing had a deep humanity and warmth that caused many listeners to say, "Listening to Pops just makes you feel good all over." In addition to being a brilliant trumpeter, he was also the father of the jazz vocal style. He toured constantly, and during the last twenty years of his life, he was one of the best-known and most-admired people in the world. His death, on July 6, 1971, was headline news around the world.

Adapted from *Marsalis on Music*.

Before you read

Predicting

The pictures below are all connected to Louis Armstrong's life. When do you think they happened? Number them from 1 (first event) to 4 (last event).

He played in a band in Chicago and became famous.

He played with bands in parades, clubs, and on steamboats.

He was arrested.

Jazz was born in New Orleans.

Reading

Scanning

Scan the text to check your predictions. Then read the whole text.

After you read

Understanding details

A Mark each sentence true (*T*) or false (*F*).

___*T*___ 1. The first jazz musicians played at the end of the nineteenth century.

_____ 2. Louis Armstrong grew up in a city where jazz was not popular.

_____ 3. A family member taught Armstrong to play his first instrument.

_____ 4. When he was in his late teens, Armstrong attended a music school.

_____ 5. Joe Oliver was important in Louis Armstrong's life.

_____ 6. Armstrong played with a famous band in Chicago.

_____ 7. Armstrong was famous only for his trumpet playing.

Understanding text organization

B These sentences can go at the end of some paragraphs. Write the number of the paragraph.

___*5*___ a. When he played, it was hard to confuse him with any other musician.

_____ b. There was a lot of sadness on that day.

_____ c. He was born at the right place at the right time.

_____ d. It was one of the most successful jazz bands at the time.

_____ e. He knew from that time that he wanted to be a musician.

Relating reading to personal experience

C Answer these questions.

1. Who are the three most famous musicians in your part of the world? What do you know about their lives?
2. What do you think a typical day is like for a professional musician? Is this a lifestyle you would like? Why or why not?
3. Are you a musician? If so, how do you feel when you are making music? If not, would you like to become one? Why or why not?

The biology of music

1 What are two things that make humans different from all other animals? One is language and the other is music. While other animals can sing — indeed, many birds do so better than a lot of people — birdsong, and the song of animals such as whales, is limited in type. No other animal has developed a musical instrument.

2 Music is strange stuff. It is clearly different from language. People can, nevertheless, use it to communicate things — especially their emotions. When combined with speech in a song, it is one of most powerful means of communication that humans have. But, biologically speaking, what is it?

3 If music is truly different from speech, then it ought to come from a distinct part of the brain. That part keeps music separate from other sounds, including language. The evidence suggests that such a part does exist.

4 People whose language-processing ability is damaged do not automatically lose their musical abilities. For example, Vissarion Shebalin, a Russian composer, suffered a stroke to the left side of his brain in 1953. After that, he could no longer speak or understand speech. He could, however, still compose music until his death ten years later. On the other hand, there are one or two cases of people who have lost their musical abilities but who can still speak and understand speech. This shows that the brain processes music and language independently.

5 A lot is known about how music works its magic. Why it does so is a different question. Geoffrey Miller, a researcher at University College, London, thinks that music and love are connected to each other. Because music requires special talent and practice, it is a way of demonstrating your fitness to be someone's mate. Singing in tune, or playing a musical instrument, requires fine muscular control. Remembering the notes demands a good memory. Getting those notes right once you have remembered them suggests a player's hearing is in top condition. Finally, the fact that much music is sung by a man to the woman he loves (or vice versa) suggests that it is, indeed, a way of showing off.

Adapted from *The Economist*.

Before you read

Check (✔) the statements you think are true.

_____ 1. People use music and speech to communicate.

_____ 2. Music comes from a distinct part of the brain.

_____ 3. When musicians have a stroke and can no longer speak, they also lose their musical abilities.

_____ 4. Music never plays a role in finding a mate.

_____ 5. Boyfriends who sing to their girlfriends are showing off.

Reading

Scan the text to check your answers. Then read the whole text.

After you read

A **What is the tone of the text? Check (✔) the correct answer.**

_____ 1. angry   _____ 3. sad

_____ 2. funny   _____ 4. serious

B **Check (✔) the correct column.**

	General statement	Specific example
1. People whose language-processing ability is damaged do not automatically lose their musical abilities.	✓	
2. After that, he could no longer speak or understand speech. He could, however, still compose music until his death ten years later.		
3. Because music requires special talent and practice, it is a way of demonstrating your fitness to be someone's mate.		
4. Singing in tune, or playing a musical instrument, requires fine muscular control.		

C **Answer these questions.**

1. What do you think animals such as birds and whales are communicating when they sing?
2. What other emotions besides love can music communicate?
3. Why do you think some people become great musicians?

Vocabulary expansion

A Complete the diagrams with the words from the box. Then add your own word to each diagram.

~~band~~	classical	guitar	oboe	tambourine
beat	composer	guitarist	orchestra	tempo
blues	cymbals	jazz	rap	trumpet
~~cello~~	drummer	Latin	rock	trumpeter
choir	drums	musician	singer	tune
clarinet	flute	note	songwriter	violin

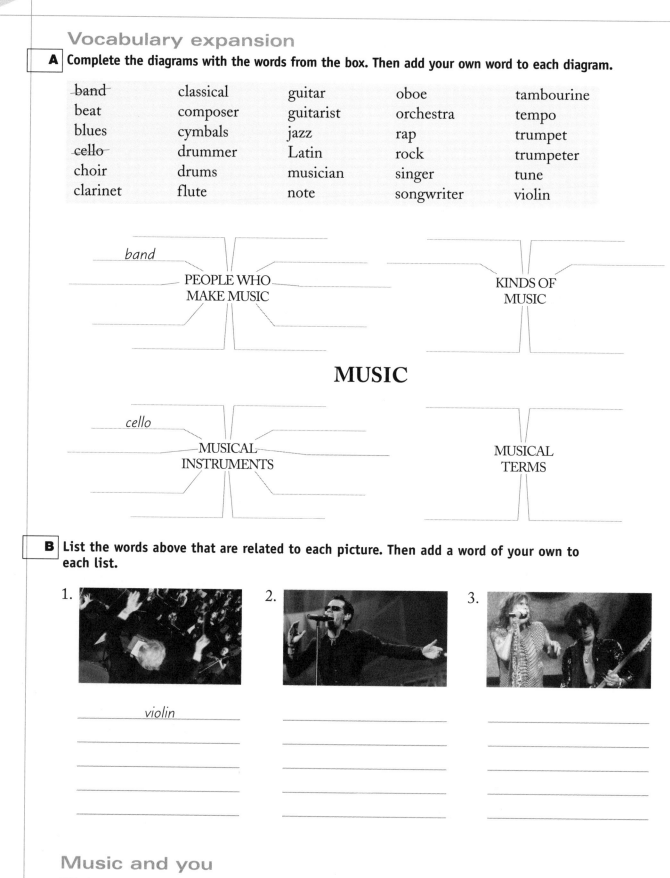

band

PEOPLE WHO
MAKE MUSIC

KINDS OF
MUSIC

MUSIC

cello

MUSICAL
INSTRUMENTS

MUSICAL
TERMS

B List the words above that are related to each picture. Then add a word of your own to each list.

1.

2.

3.

violin

Music and you

With a partner, make a list of the five most famous songs or singers ever recorded. Then join another pair and compare your lists.

UNIT 2 Money

You are going to read three texts about money. First, answer the questions in the boxes.

Dangers in shopping

Read about people who just can't stop shopping, and for whom shopping has become a problem.

1. Do you know anyone who shops too much?
2. How can you avoid buying things you don't need?

How to be a millionaire

Are millionaires different from ordinary people? What is the secret to becoming a millionaire? Find out in this magazine article.

1. Would you like to be a millionaire? Why or why not?
2. What do you think you have to do to become a millionaire?

Pity the poor lottery winner

In this magazine article you will find out what happens to people who win a lottery. It doesn't always mean good news for the winner.

1. How would your life change if you won the lottery?
2. What are some unpleasant results of winning the lottery?

Vocabulary

To find out the meanings of the words in *italics*, work with another student, ask your teacher, or use a dictionary. Then check (✔) the statements that are true about you.

_____ 1. I don't expect to *make* a lot of *money* in the future.

_____ 2. I *spend* money as soon as I get it.

_____ 3. I'm very *frugal*. I *save* as much as I can and don't spend more than I need to.

_____ 4. I think that spending money is more satisfying than *earning* it.

_____ 5. I plan to *make a fortune* in the future and will work as hard as I can to do so.

_____ 6. Happiness comes from within yourself and not from *wealth* and *possessions*.

_____ 7. I never go into *debt*.

Dangers in shopping

1 Feeling lonely? Why not go to the mall? You'll find plenty of company, and yes, a new pair of shoes or maybe even a new computer game. It's quick and effortless; and you don't need special equipment. You just get in your car and drive to a store. They're everywhere, and they're open 24 hours in any weather.

2 Most people think of shopping as something we do when we need to buy things, but some people shop for different reasons. In fact, if you're like many people today, shopping is your favorite hobby, something you can easily do to change your mood. You might feel great, but if you are not careful, the total on your credit card bills will soon be more than you have in your bank account.

3 Because shopping is so enjoyable and convenient, it can be addictive. "People get into the dangerous habit of spending money to try to feel good. They become trapped in a cycle of self-defeating behavior that leads to debt and dissatisfaction," says Fred E. Waddell, author of *Money Mastery in Minutes a Day*.

4 How do you know if you are a compulsive spender, and not just someone who has spent more than you should have this month? There is no easy answer. But ask yourself this: Do you have clothes in your closet that you never wear or that still have the price tags on them? Do you ever hide your purchases from your family? Beware, these are some of the warning signs, says Dr. Waddell.

5 According to him, most compulsive spenders are unaware of their habits or strongly deny them. Compulsive spenders prefer to avoid the issues that force them to shop, so the problem is not just that they spend more than they earn. Spending problems may result from deep personal problems that compulsive spenders have. However, they are not fully aware of these problems.

6 Some spontaneous spending is natural: flowers to brighten a rainy day, or a treat for a job well done. To be spontaneous means to act without planning. However, a compulsive spender will shop in response to stress and follow a real physical urge to go out and spend money. When this type of spending causes serious problems for you and your family, you have a compulsive-spending problem.

READING TIP Sometimes the meaning of a word is explained in the text. For example, the text explains the meaning of *spontaneous*: "To be spontaneous means to act without planning."

Adapted from aol.thewhiz.com/brm/

Before you read

Thinking about personal experience

Are you a compulsive shopper? Take this shopping habits quiz to find out.

	Yes	Sometimes	No
1. Do you shop just to make yourself feel good?			
2. Do you shop when you feel stress?			
3. Do you buy clothes that you never wear?			
4. Do you ever hide your purchases from your family?			
5. Do you plan what you want to buy?			

Reading

Scanning

Scan the text to find out if you have a shopping problem. Then read the whole text.

After you read

Guessing meaning from context

A **Find the words in *italics* in the reading. Then match each word with its meaning.**

_e_ 1. *lonely* (par. 1)   a. describes something that people cannot stop doing

____ 2. *company* (par. 1)   b. not knowing something

____ 3. *addictive* (par. 3)   c. something special

____ 4. *beware* (par. 4)   d. other people with you

____ 5. *unaware* (par. 5)   e. feeling sad because you are by yourself

____ 6. *treat* (par. 6)   f. be careful

Understanding details

B **Circle the correct answers.**

1. According to the article, most people think of shopping as something to do
   a. when they are lonely.
   b. when they need to buy things.
2. Compulsive shoppers buy things because
   a. they need to feel good.
   b. shopping is their favorite hobby.
3. Most compulsive shoppers
   a. are happy to talk about their problem.
   b. don't like to discuss their problem.
4. Spontaneous spending is usually
   a. harmless.
   b. dangerous.

Relating reading to personal experience

C **Answer these questions.**

1. In what ways are you similar to a compulsive shopper? How are you different?
2. What is the last thing that you bought spontaneously? Why did you buy it?
3. Why do you think compulsive shoppers try to hide their habit?

HOW TO BE A MILLIONAIRE

1 When you think of millionaires, do you think of people wearing diamonds and driving expensive cars? Actually, the rich are far more likely to be wearing old jeans and driving an old pickup truck. They don't try to look different from ordinary people, say authors Thomas Stanley and William Danko in their book, *The Millionaire Next Door.* They surveyed America's millionaires and found that the main secret to wealth was modest spending. "Anyone can be wealthy if they make a plan, are frugal, and work hard," says Stanley. Here is what else they found.

2 Eighty percent of millionaires in America made their fortunes in one generation. They didn't inherit their money from their family. Most of them own a business. Two-thirds of them are self-employed, often in blue-collar industries, where you don't need to wear a suit. They are roofing contractors, dry cleaners, and scrap-metal dealers. These people were not the A students in high school; they were the B and C students.

3 Women are less likely to become millionaires than men, unless it's through marriage. There are far more men than women in the high-paying jobs in the U.S. — physicians, lawyers, optometrists; and the women who go into these professions earn much less than the men. Moreover, women in all professions tend to get more financial help from their parents.

4 There are not a lot of millionaires in the white-collar professions. If you're a doctor, lawyer, or stockbroker, you have to look wealthy and successful, like your clients. You're under pressure to spend a lot of money, and that eats away at your savings.

5 The typical millionaire earns $130,000 a year and saves about 20 percent of it annually. They spend time managing their money and planning their financial future.

6 Even those who don't earn a lot of money can become millionaires. People don't understand how little money it could take to become a millionaire. If people who drank three cans of soda a day for 46 years had invested that money in soft drink company stocks instead, they'd be millionaires.

Adapted from *People Weekly.*

Before you read

Check (✔) the statements you think are true.

_____ 1. Most millionaires drive expensive cars.

_____ 2. Millionaires spend their money carefully.

_____ 3. Most millionaires get their money from their parents.

_____ 4. Most millionaires are self-employed and own businesses like dry cleaners.

_____ 5. Most millionaires were not great students.

_____ 6. There are more female than male millionaires.

_____ 7. Doctors and lawyers are usually millionaires.

Reading

Scan the text to check your answers. Then read the whole text.

After you read

A **Here are the questions the authors answered. Write the paragraph number next to the question that paragraph answers.**

_6_ a. How can someone who makes the average U.S. salary save enough to become a millionaire?

_____ b. How much do millionaires tend to save each year?

_____ c. Why aren't there more millionaires in the white-collar professions?

_____ d. Are women less likely than men to become millionaires?

_____ e. In which professions do most millionaires make their money?

B **Complete the statements.**

1. Millionaires are far _____less_____ likely to wear expensive clothes and drive new cars.

2. _____ percent of millionaires inherited money from their parents or grandparents.

3. _____ of millionaires work for someone else.

4. Men are _____ likely to become millionaires than women.

5. Men in high-paying jobs earn much _____ than women.

6. There are only a _____ millionaires in the white-collar professions.

7. In the United States, far _____ women than men have the jobs that pay well.

C **Answer these questions.**

1. Do you think the advice in the article would help you in your country? Why or why not?

2. Why do you think some wealthy people dress like ordinary people?

3. Why do you think there are far more poor people than wealthy people in the world?

Pity the poor lottery winner

1 Most of us think that if we won millions in a lottery, it would solve all our problems. In fact, winning the lottery often brings big trouble. Take the case of Cindy, who won a $2.5 million prize ten years ago. As with many winners, at first she was excited. She soon got a shock, however, when her friend said, "What right did you have to win?" Cindy had hardly ever bought lottery tickets; her friend had been buying tickets for years and really needed money. She had even planned to go with Cindy to buy those tickets; but at the last minute, she couldn't go. Somehow she felt Cindy had cheated her. Other unpleasant surprises came from her own family. Her mother thought Cindy ought to share the prize money with her sister. When Cindy disagreed, she and her mother didn't speak for six years.

2 William "Bud" Post won $16.2 million in the lottery and was broke five years later. What was more, his brother was in jail for hiring someone to murder Bud and his sixth wife for the lottery money. Post said he was happier before he won, when all he had was a job with a circus. After he won the money, friends and family begged or borrowed money from him, several businesses he started up failed, and an ex-girlfriend sued him.

3 Of course, there are happy winners too. They tend to have close family ties. Many of them also have strong religious faith and a firm sense of who they are. Lydia Neufeld won $17 million in 1990. She and her husband, Dave, bought a church for their Spanish-speaking community. Dave gave his family business to his employees.

4 But what about Paul McNabb? He was a baker who became Maryland's first lottery millionaire. He received kidnap threats to his children, thieves broke into his house, and he lost the work he liked. Worst of all, he also lost trust in other people — the loss "of being human." In spite of all this, McNabb said he wouldn't give the money back. He enjoyed it. But would he do it again — relive those 20 years as a winner? "No way," he laughed.

Adapted from *The New York Times Magazine*.

Before you read

Look at the title on the opposite page and the words and phrases below. Find out the meanings of any words you don't know. Then check (✔) those you think you will read in the text.

_____ 1. *cheated*	_____ 5. *lots of parties*
_____ 2. *made everyone happy*	_____ 6. *shared winnings with family and friends*
_____ 3. *was broke*	_____ 7. *kidnap threats*
_____ 4. *murder*	_____ 8. *thieves broke in*

Reading

Scan the text to check your predictions. Then read the whole text.

After you read

A Check (✔) the correct column. There is only one main idea.

	Main idea	Not the main idea	Not in the text
1. how winning money can be a good experience		✓	
2. how much money people won			
3. how winning money can create problems			
4. how lottery winners spend their money			
5. how to improve your chances of winning			

B Who had these experiences? Complete the statements with *Cindy*, *William*, or *Paul*.

1. ___William___ was broke five years after winning the lottery.
2. _____ had a friend who felt cheated by him or her.
3. _____ had businesses that were not successful.
4. _____ no longer trusted other people.
5. _____ 's children were in danger.
6. _____ didn't talk to a family member for years.
7. _____ had a family member that tried to kill him or her.
8. _____ had friends that were always asking for money.

C Answer these questions.

1. Why do you think winning a lottery can have a bad effect on a family?
2. Do you think Cindy's friend was wrong? Why or why not?
3. If you won money in a lottery, would you share it with anyone? If so, whom?

Vocabulary expansion

Complete the crossword puzzle with words from the unit. The numbers in parentheses after the clues below show the reading in which the word appears.

Across

2. Careful in the use of money (2)
3. People with millions of dollars (2)
7. What people with lottery tickets want to do (3)
8. When you owe money, you are in _____. (1)
9. People want a _____-paying job. (2)
10. Put money into something to make money (2)
11. Get money by working (2)
12. Try to get money from someone by going to court (3)
13. A lot of money (2)

Down

1. Doing something without control (1)
2. Connected with money (2)
4. To use money is to _____ it. (1)
5. Rich (2)
6. When you have no money, you are _____. (3)
10. To get money from a family member after his or her death (2)
12. Keep money to use later (2)
14. To have or possess (2)

Money and you

Do a survey of people's money habits. First, come up with ten questions. Then ask your classmates or friends and family. Report your findings to the class.

Example: What is something you do to save money?

UNIT 3 Work

You are going to read three texts about work. First, answer the questions in the boxes.

Your first job

In this magazine article you will find out what happens to people when they start their first job. How does the job change them?

1. What work experience do you have?
2. What do you think are some difficulties people have when they start a new job?

Job satisfaction

Why are some people happy with their jobs and others are not? This newspaper article gives the result of a poll on the subject.

1. Do you think most people you know are satisfied with their jobs? If so, why? If not, why not?
2. What kind of job would you be most happy doing?

Are you a workaholic?

This newspaper article describes compulsive workers and the problems these people have.

1. How many hours a week do people in your country work?
2. Do you know people who work more than the average number of hours? Do they need to work so many hours or do they want to?

Vocabulary

Find out the meanings of the words in *italics*. Then think of a job you would like to have, and answer the questions about this job. (Note: If you do not know the answer, write *I don't know*.)

1. What is the *salary* for a *starting position*?
2. What are the *job requirements*?
3. Is there a *flexible schedule*?
4. Is there a lot of contact with *co-workers*?
5. Is *teamwork* a big part of this job?
6. Are there good opportunities for *advancement*?

Your FIRST job

1   Learning what to expect from your first job is a lot like learning to drive a car or ride a bicycle. Instructors can give you a lot of advice, but in the end, you just have to figure it out for yourself. Here are some realities of the working world that often surprise people who are beginning their first job:

2   "It's a lot more dog-eat-dog than I'd expected. You see people come and go who you thought were doing just fine in their jobs. Everyone acts friendly, but you realize that nobody's going to keep you on just because you're a good person." —Peter

3   "As soon as you start working, personal errands become the biggest hassle. I can never get to the gym; I plan my evening around picking up my dry cleaning. How did people get by before 24-hour banking and 24-hour groceries?" —Jennifer

4   "I was shocked to find that some of the people I worked for treated me with less respect than they did others above me. They assumed I had a substandard intelligence because I was in a starting position." —Kelly

5   "The first time I addressed someone much older than me, he said, 'Mr. Baker's my dad. I'm Bill.' I had to flip a mental switch to get used to working on the same level as people older than me." —Lisa

6   "It's very satisfying to realize that you're working because someone really needs something done, not so that you'll get a good grade." —Jason

7   "Teamwork is something you rarely experience in school, but it's something my office really emphasizes. It's not just to your benefit if you have a good idea, it's to everyone's — which means that people are much more patient when listening to what you have to say than they were in a college seminar." —Adam

8   "Before I started working, I'd get dressed in the morning and then not think about how I looked again. When you're in a job where you're working with the public, you're constantly making sure you look neat and put together throughout the day. . . ." —Kate

Adapted from *Glamour.*

Before you read

What is most difficult about starting your first job? Number these things from 1 (most difficult) to 6 (least difficult).

_____ working well with others   _____ getting respect

_____ knowing how to dress   _____ working with older people

_____ managing one's personal life   _____ dealing with competition

Reading

Scan the text to find out what people said about their first jobs. Write the speaker's name next to the problem. Then read the whole text.

1. working well with others   _Adam_   4. getting respect   _____

2. knowing how to dress   _____   5. talking with older people   _____

3. managing one's personal life _____   6. dealing with competition   _____

After you read

A **Who felt good about their first job? Complete the chart with the speakers' names.**

Not good	Neutral	Good
Peter		

B **Find the words in _italics_ in the reading. Circle the meaning of each word.**

1. _dog-eat-dog_ (Peter)   (a.) people do anything to succeed
                            b. people work with dogs

2. _errands_ (Jennifer)   a. a special job, usually at the office
                            b. a short trip, especially to buy something

3. _hassle_ (Jennifer)   a. the most important part of a job
                            b. a situation that causes difficulty

4. _substandard_ (Kelly)   a. lower than usual
                            b. higher than usual

5. _addressed_ (Lisa)   a. wrote someone's name on an envelope
                            b. spoke to someone

6. _benefit_ (Adam)   a. extra money someone gets for doing good work
                            b. something that may help someone to be successful

C **Answer these questions.**

1. What advice would you give to people beginning their first job?
2. Do you think women and men have different difficulties when they start a new job? If so, what are they?
3. Do people who work in an office have different problems than people who do other kinds of work? If so, how are the challenges different?

Job satisfaction

1   Why do most people choose to stay with their current employer? The answer usually depends on their age, life circumstances, and personal motivations. A recent poll on our website asked the same question.

2   The top reason for staying on the job was nature of the work and job satisfaction. Coming in a close second was flexible schedule and work-life balance. Next was work environment and corporate culture, followed by advancement opportunity and personal growth. Salary and benefits were the least important.

3   Is it unusual that salary comes in last on this list? Not really. Salary and benefits do not usually make it into the top three reasons for job satisfaction on such surveys. Most people know they could make more money elsewhere, but it's not enough to get them to leave a job they like.

4   Advancement doesn't rank at the top of the list, either. That's probably because so many people think that moving up can make life on the job more unpleasant. The only thing one gets in return is more money.

5   So what creates job satisfaction? One typical answer is "I like to be challenged." People who say this like to work toward goals. They like new challenging assignments so that they can test their skills and creativity.

6   Another typical answer is "I like to feel I'm making a contribution." Many people get a sense of community when they are working with a group of co-workers toward a common goal. It is very important for them to have close, friendly relationships with co-workers, and they thrive when others praise their work and appreciate their efforts.

7   Finally, there are those who say "I get satisfaction from a job well done." Such people love the technical work they do; they feel proud of the results of their efforts. These people have high standards of quality and work best when they have control over a project. They thrive when others know about the work they have done.

8   Ultimately, the main reason people work is to earn money, but it is not money that gives them satisfaction. Offer employees something more, and you are likely to get more from them.

Adapted from *Milwaukee Journal Sentinel.*

Before you read

**Why do you think most people stay in their jobs? Number the reasons from
1 (most important) to 5 (least important).**

	Advancement opportunity and personal growth
	Flexible schedule and work-life balance
	Nature of the work and job satisfaction
	Work environment and corporate culture
	Salary and benefits

Reading

Scan the text to find out why most people stay in their jobs. Then read the whole text.

After you read

A **Who do you think the text was written for? Check (✔) the correct answer.**

_____ 1. students _____ 2. workers _____ 3. managers

B **What creates job satisfaction? Check (✔) the three main reasons.**

✓ 1. People like to be challenged.

_____ 2. People like new challenging assignments so that they test their skills and creativity.

_____ 3. People like to feel they're making a contribution.

_____ 4. People thrive when others praise their work and appreciate their efforts.

_____ 5. People love the work they do; they feel proud of the results of their efforts.

_____ 6. People get satisfaction from a job well done.

C **Compare the meaning of each pair of sentences. Write same (S) or different (D).**

_D_ 1. Why do most people choose to stay with their current employer?
Why do most people change jobs?

_____ 2. The top reason for staying on the job was job satisfaction.
More people chose job satisfaction than any other answer.

_____ 3. Most people know they could make more money elsewhere.
Most people know there are other places that pay better salaries.

_____ 4. They are happy with the results of their efforts.
They are happy that they succeeded.

D **Answer these questions.**

1. Which of these statements are true about you or about someone you know?
I like to be challenged. / I like to feel I'm making a contribution. / I get
satisfaction from a job well done.
2. Is there a goal you are currently working toward? If so, what is it?
3. What should you do if you are not satisfied with your job?

Are you a workaholic?

1 Do you think about work all the time? Do you work long hours, far beyond the requirements of the job? Are you anxious when you're not at work?

2 If you answered "yes," then you might be a workaholic, a person who is compulsively addicted to work.

3 How can that be, addicted to work? In truth, you can abuse anything — food, exercise. Work addiction is just one more form of compulsive behavior. It keeps us constantly busy and stops us from looking inside ourselves. "Like other addictions, you are seeking a way of not having to look at or feel things or just to self-medicate to take care of pain, anxiety, or feelings," says Janet Salyer, a professional counselor. "Workaholics put the job before family, friends, and their own health. Even if they're spending time with their families, their mind is on work."

4 Take note: There is a difference between hard work and compulsive work. Hard work enriches your life even if it includes some periods of long hours and extra work. Compulsive work, on the other hand, prevents you from leading a full life.

5 But we live in a society that rewards compulsive work, and we get applauded for keeping long hours and taking on more and more responsibilities. Being called a workaholic is often not taken as an insult.

6 "Our society in some ways reinforces and rewards workaholism. Sometimes it is subtle, but there is a lot of recognition given to people for being extremely busy. It is almost like equating someone's value with how busy they are," Salyer says.

7 A client of Salyer's said her co-workers often came in on Monday mornings and talked about how many hours they had worked during the weekend. The people who didn't work on Saturday or Sunday were viewed as less interested in their jobs.

8 "Some organizations reinforce overwork," she says. "Learn to relax and not neglect your private life."

READING TIP

Sometimes it is not necessary to know the exact meaning of a word to understand a text. It is often enough to know whether a word has a positive or negative meaning. For example, you may not need to know exactly what *enriches* means. It may be enough to know that it has a positive meaning.

Adapted from *The Nashville Tennessean.*

Before you read

Check (✔) the information you think you will read about in the text.

_____ 1. what it means to be a workaholic

_____ 2. how an addiction to work is different from an addiction to food

_____ 3. how hard work is different from compulsive work

_____ 4. why some people become workaholics

_____ 5. what workaholics can do about their problem

Reading

Scan the text to check your predictions. Then read the whole text.

After you read

A | **Find the answers to the questions. Then underline them in the text.**

1. What are the characteristics of a workaholic?

   (par. 1) Do you think about work all the time? Do you work long hours, far

   beyond the requirements of the job? Are you anxious when you're not at work?

2. How is an addiction to work similar to an addiction to food?
3. How are hard work and compulsive work different?
4. How does American society help create workaholics?
5. How is an addiction to work different from other addictions?
6. What do some people think of workers who don't work long hours?

B | **Find the words in _italics_ in the reading. Do they have a positive or negative meaning? Complete the chart.**

abuse (par. 3)	_insult_ (par. 5)	_recognition_ (par. 6)
anxious (par. 1)	_overwork_ (par. 8)	_rewards_ (par. 5 and 6)
applauded (par. 5)	_pain_ (par. 3)	_value_ (par. 6)
enriches (par. 4)		

Positive	Negative
applauded	_abuse_

C | **Answer these questions.**

1. Do you know people who are addicted to work? How do you know they are not just hard workers?
2. Are people in some types of jobs more likely to become workaholics? If so, why?
3. What are some things workaholics can do to overcome their problem?

Vocabulary expansion

A Mark each idiom positive in meaning (+), negative in meaning (−), or neutral (✔).

_____−_____ 1. *dog-eat-dog:* very competitive

_____ 2. *going places:* said of someone who is already achieving success in their work and is probably going to become even more successful

_____ 3. *line of work:* the type of work someone does

_____ 4. *not pull your weight:* not work as hard as everyone else who is working on a task with you

_____ 5. *up-and-coming:* said of someone or something that is probably going to be successful in the future

_____ 6. *will go a long way:* said of people who will be very successful in their work, especially because they have shown ability in something

_____ 7. *work like a dog:* work very hard

B Complete each dialog with an idiom from exercise A.

1. A: You can't steal his ideas. It's not right.

   B: Well, it's a __dog-eat-dog__ world. That's the only way I'll succeed.

2. A: Why do you want to change jobs?

   B: Because I _____, and my boss still is never happy.

3. A: What's your _____ ?

   B: I work for an insurance company.

4. A: I understand you and Joanne are not satisfied with my work.

   B: That's right. We think you do _____. You don't finish things on time, and then someone else has to finish for you.

5. A: What do you think of the new technician?

   B: I think she _____. I know she just started here, but she seems to have a lot of talent.

6. A: Who are Tyler Golders and Tina Yono?

   B: They're _____ actors. They're still young, and they've already won many prizes.

Work and you

What kind of work do you think your classmates would be good at? Work with another student. Discuss what kinds of jobs you think would be suitable for each person and why. Then tell the rest of the class about some of your choices.

UNIT

4 Sports

You are going to read three texts about sports. First, answer the questions in the boxes.

READING 1

Do pro athletes make too much money?

This magazine article deals with how much professional athletes in the United States earn in comparison with other professions.

1. Who is your favorite athlete? Do you know how much he or she earns?
2. Are athletes worth a lot of money in your country? If so, who is worth the most?

READING 2

Extreme sports

In this newspaper article, find out why extreme sports are becoming more and more popular.

1. Are you an adventurous person, or are you afraid to take risks?
2. What are some examples of dangerous sports? Why do you think people like to take part in these sports?

READING 3

Frequently asked questions about the ancient Olympic Games

Read from this website to learn about, among other things, who could compete in the ancient Olympics and what the prizes were.

1. Do you enjoy watching the Olympic Games? Why or why not?
2. Would you rather see the athletic skill of the world's greatest athletes or see athletes from your country win?

Vocabulary

Find out the meanings of the words in *italics*. Then check (✔) the statements that are true about you.

_____ 1. I don't know of any professional athlete who has *cheated*.

_____ 2. I like to *compete* in *team* sports.

_____ 3. I'm a soccer *fan*.

_____ 4. I know the *rules* of all the major sports in my country.

_____ 5. I have been the *victor* in many games I have played.

DO PRO ATHLETES MAKE TOO MUCH MONEY?

Profession	Average salary (per year)	Minimum starting salary
basketball player	$2.2 million	$220,000
baseball player	$1.37 million	$109,000
hockey player	$892,000	$125,000
football player	$795,000	$131,000

1 In contrast:

- The average pay for classroom teachers in the United States is $38,000 per year. At that rate, a teacher would need a little more than 27 years to make $1 million — less than half what a basketball player makes, on average, in just one year.

- The average pay for firefighters in the United States is around $40,000.

- The starting salary for police officers in the United States is around $29,000.

Do athletes deserve more money than firefighters or teachers — people who hold what many consider to be more valuable jobs?

2 YES! They're worth it!

Many people, including sports fans, say athletes deserve high salaries.

- Sports fans are willing to pay increasingly higher ticket prices and watch TV sports events in large numbers. That means more money is going to the teams.

- There are only a few of these superstar athletes, and the fans' demand for them is high. The demand raises the price of athletes' services.

- Some also say that athletes are paid fairly when compared with others in the entertainment industry. It is not unusual for movie stars to make between $15 million and $20 million per movie.

- "People forget that sports is entertainment," says Leonard Armato, a sports agent.

- Top athletes believe they are worth a lot of money because they make millions of dollars for team owners. The team owners make money from ticket sales, television deals, and sales of team T-shirts, caps, and other items.

3 NO! They are not worth it!

People who think pro athletes are overpaid say other, more important professions are more worthy.

- Police officers, firefighters, and doctors save lives — sometimes while risking their own — for a fraction of what sports stars make. Soldiers defend and protect the country, sometimes giving their lives. Teachers are responsible for educating the country's children.

- The president of the United States earns $200,000 a year. Should the leader of the country make less money per year than a basketball player who is just starting out?

Adapted from *Current Events*.

Using previous knowledge

Before you read

How much is it? Change these amounts from U.S. dollars to the currency of your country.

1. $2.2 million _____   5. $200,000 _____

2. $1.37 million _____   6. $40,000 _____

3. $892,000 _____   7. $38,000 _____

4. $795,000 _____   8. $29,000 _____

Reading

Scanning

Scan the text to find out which professions earn the amounts of money above. Then read the whole text.

After you read

Understanding text organization

A Which is the best description of the article? Check (✔) the correct answer.

_____ 1. The article begins with facts and then gives the opinion of the writer.

_____ 2. The article is about the writer's opinion.

_____ 3. The article begins with facts. Then it explains the opinions of different groups of people.

_____ 4. The article has the writer's opinion and the opinions of different groups of people.

Distinguishing arguments

B Circle the answers that are *not* mentioned in the text.

1. Why do some people think athletes deserve so much money?
   a. They make a lot of money for their teams.
   b. They work very hard to become professional athletes.
   c. Movie stars make more money than professional athletes.
   d. Fans are willing pay to see the superstar athletes.

2. Why do some people think athletes make too much money?
   a. Athletes do not usually have a lot of education.
   b. People who risk their lives do more valuable work than athletes.
   c. People who do important jobs should make more money than athletes.
   d. Nobody needs millions of dollars to live.

Relating reading to personal experience

C Answer these questions.

1. Which of the arguments in the article do you agree with? Which do you disagree with?
2. Do you think professional athletes make too much money? Why or why not?
3. Should money earned reflect the importance of a job to society? For example, should a firefighter make more than a businessperson? Why or why not?

Extreme sports

1 Rock climbing, white-water rafting, and skydiving used to be considered dangerous sports, suitable for only a few bold people — the unusually fit. Not so today, when it is common for families to take up such activities.

2 Why do people want to take part in dangerous activities? Some experts say it's the innate human desire to test the limits of their courage and physical abilities.

3 Sports psychologist Frank Farley of Temple University in Philadelphia calls people who do dangerous sports "Type T"

people. They are thrill seekers and risk takers. Farley has been studying such people for 35 years. "They're the mountain climbers, the hang-gliders, the people who sail around the world in a ten-foot sailboat," says the sports psychologist.

4 What are the reasons behind the popularity of high-risk activities? Some say it's due to more wealth, the development of

high-tech equipment, and even the absence of traditional risks such as war. Others argue that the self-centeredness and relative ease of modern life are part of the reason. In addition, thrill seekers want to display a youthful, rebellious attitude, whether they're 16 or 46.

5 "Much of that has to do with the affluence and boredom of America's upper and middle classes," wrote Andrew Exum in his college newspaper. "Many Americans today can simply afford to do things that used to be done only by professional adventurers."

6 "But being able to pay for a trip to the top of Everest — the going rate is about $60,000 — doesn't explain why you would risk your life and actually go. Many Americans seem to need to take risks and be adventurous. If given the opportunity to take risks, we will."

7 Farley says such activities almost always involve individual expression — even creativity. "I don't know how extreme sports are going to end," Farley says. "They're hot and getting hotter."

READING TIP

If you know one form of a word — for example, the adjective *easy* — you can guess the meaning of another form of the word — for example, the noun *ease* (par. 4).

Adapted from *The Christian Science Monitor.*

Before you read

Look at the pictures on the opposite page and the phrases below. Find out the meanings of any words you don't know. Then check (✔) those you think you will read in the text.

_____ 1. *unusually fit*   _____ 7. *famous athletes*

_____ 2. *element of danger*   _____ 8. *high-risk activities*

_____ 3. *exercise and talent*   _____ 9. *advice of doctors*

_____ 4. *desire to test courage*   _____ 10. *affluence and boredom*

_____ 5. *physical abilities*   _____ 11. *high-tech equipment*

_____ 6. *fear of accidents*   _____ 12. *hundreds of years*

Reading

Scan the text to check your predictions. Then read the whole text.

After you read

A **Find the words in *italics* in the reading. Circle the meaning of each word.**

1. *Bold* people **fear /(don't fear)** doing something dangerous. (par. 1)
2. Something *innate* is something you **are born with / learn.** (par. 2)
3. *Thrill seekers* are looking for **a quiet / an exciting** life. (par. 3)
4. A person who is *self-centered* has a **high / low** opinion of himself or herself. (par. 4)
5. If you are *rebellious*, you try to be **different from / similar to** others. (par. 4)
6. If something is *hot*, it is getting **more / less** popular. (par. 7)

B **Check (✔) the statements that are true.**

✔ 1. The people who did extreme sports 30 years ago are similar to the people who do them nowadays.

_____ 2. High-tech equipment makes extreme sports less dangerous.

_____ 3. People who have difficult lives are not interested in extreme sports.

_____ 4. People who do extreme sports are young.

_____ 5. It can cost a lot of money to do extreme sports.

_____ 6. There have always been people who want to take a lot of risks.

C **Answer these questions.**

1. Imagine a trip to the top of Mount Everest. If you had the money, would you like to go? Why or why not?
2. Which of the extreme sports mentioned in the article would you like to try? Which would you never do? Why?
3. Do you think that only Americans enjoy extreme sports? Do you know someone who does extreme sports? If so, do you think this person likes to take risks? Is this person wealthy or bored with modern life?

Frequently asked questions about the ancient Olympic Games

1 Today, the Olympic Games are the world's largest show of athletic skill and competitive spirit. This was also true in the ancient Greek world. The ancient Olympic Games were part of a major religious festival honoring Zeus, the most important Greek god. The Games were the biggest event in their world, and were the scene of political rivalries between people from different parts of the Greek world.

Who could compete in the Olympics?

2 The Olympics were open to any free-born Greek in the world. There were separate men's and boys' divisions for the events. The judges divided athletes into the boys' or men's divisions according to physical size, strength and age.

3 Women were not allowed to compete in the Games. However, they could enter equestrian events as the owner of a chariot team or an individual horse and win that way.

Were women allowed at the Olympics?

4 Not only were women not permitted to compete, but married women were also forbidden to attend the games, under penalty of death. (Unmarried women were allowed to attend.)

What prizes did the Olympic winners get?

5 A winner received a crown made from olive leaves, and he could have a statue of himself set up in Olympia.

6 Although he did not receive money at the Olympics, the winner got much of the same treatment from his home city as a modern-day sports celebrity. His success increased the fame and reputation of his community in the Greek world. It was common for winners to eat all their meals at public expense. In addition, they would also have front-row seats at the theater and other public festivals. One city even built a private gym for their Olympic-wrestling champion to exercise in.

Who were the Olympic judges?

7 Unlike the modern Olympics, judges did not come from all over the world. They were Eleans, or from Elis, a local region that included Olympia.

8 Even though the judges were all Eleans, local Elean Greeks were still allowed to compete in the Olympics. The Elean people had such a reputation for fairness that an Elean cheating at the Games was a shock to other Greeks.

What was the penalty for cheating?

9 The judges fined anyone who violated the rules. The money was used for statues of Zeus.

Adapted from *www.perseus.tufts.edu/Olympics/sports.html*.

Before you read

How much do you know about the ancient Olympics? Answer these questions.

1. Who could compete in the Olympics? _____

2. Who were the Olympic judges? _____

3. What prizes did the Olympic winners get? _____

4. What was the penalty for cheating? _____

5. Were women allowed at the Olympics? _____

Reading

Scan the text to check your answers. Then read the whole text.

After you read

A **Find the words in the text related to the words in column A. Then match the words in column B with their meanings in column C.**

A	B	C
1. *athlete n.* (par. 1)	*athletic* *adj.*	a. (the quality of) following the rules
2. *divide v.* (par. 2)	*n.*	b. (the state of) being very well-known
3. *strong adj.* (par. 2)	*n.*	c. the cost of something
4. *famous adj.* (par. 6)	*n.*	d. trained or skilled in a sport
5. *expensive adj.* (par. 6)	*n.*	e. physical power
6. *fair adj.* (par. 8)	*n.*	f. separate

B **Read the sentences about the modern Olympics. Then write sentences about the ancient Olympics.**

1. Nationalism, commerce, and politics are part of the modern Olympics.

   Religion and politics were part of the ancient Olympics.

2. Women compete in a lot of different events in the modern Olympics.

   _____

3. Women attend the different events in the modern Olympics.

   _____

4. Winners in the modern Olympics receive medals as prizes.

   _____

5. Judges in the modern Olympics come from all over the world.

   _____

6. Anyone who cheats in the modern Olympics has to leave the games.

   _____

C **Answer these questions.**

1. Which Olympic events do you like the best?

2. What do you think ancient Greeks would find most surprising about the modern games?

3. Is it important for the Olympic Games to continue? Why or why not?

Vocabulary expansion

A The words in each column refer to a sport. Write the name of the sport under the box.

1.	2.	3.	4.	5.	6.
a ballpark	a basket	a ball	a ball	a court	a lane
a bat	a court	a club	a field	a match	an official
catch	a game	a course	a game	a net	a race
a homerun	a point	a hole	a goal	a point	run
an inning	a referee	swing	kick	a racket	running shoes
an umpire	shoot	a tee	a referee	swing	a track

baseball ....

B Complete the blanks with words from the columns. Write at least three words that refer to:

1. a place where people play a sport

   a ballpark, a court, a field

2. equipment that people use to play a sport

   ....

3. a person who makes sure the players in a game follow the rules

   ....

4. something that players need to score in order to win

   ....

5. an action that players do in different sports

   ....

6. a way that a sport is divided or organized

   ....

C Now write a similar list of words for another sport you know. Can other students guess the sport you chose?

Sports and you

Plan the sports page of a newspaper. Decide the following:

1. How many articles will appear on the page?
2. What will the subject of each article be?
3. What should the headline of each article be?

UNIT 5 Weather

You are going to read three texts about weather. First, answer the questions in the boxes.

READING 1

Keeping an eye on the weather

Find out how meteorologists make their predictions about the weather.

1. How often do you read or listen to weather forecasts?
2. What do meteorologists use to predict the weather?

READING 2

Nature's weather forecasters

Learn about changes in wildlife behavior when the weather is about to change.

1. How do you think changes in weather affect animals?
2. Do you think changes in weather affect humans or animals more? Why do you think so?

READING 3

Could you survive a natural disaster?

What can you do to prepare your home against a disaster? This magazine article gives you the information you need to know.

1. What natural disasters are most common in your part of the world?
2. What can you do to prepare your home in case there is a natural disaster?

Vocabulary

Find out the meanings of the words in the box. Then write each word under the correct heading.

air pressure	a flood	a hurricane	the South Pole	temperature
the equator	humidity	the North Pole	a storm	a tornado

PLACES ON THE PLANET EARTH   **WEATHER PROBLEMS**   **WEATHER MEASUREMENTS**

_____   _____   _____
_____   _____   _____
_____   _____   _____
_____   _____   _____
_____   _____   _____

Keeping an **eye** on the weather

1 Weather forecasters don't just look out the window to prepare the report you see on TV or hear on the radio. They use a sophisticated weather information network located all over — and above — the globe. Satellites orbit Earth constantly. Planes and balloons ascend daily to collect data. Weather stations in almost every country on the earth contribute data.

2 As you've noticed, forecasters sometimes make mistakes. That's because a forecast is only a prediction. It is based on what's happening now. However, nature doesn't always follow a predictable pattern, so a forecast is only an educated guess, not a guarantee.

Weather satellite

3 Weather satellites remain in fixed positions 22,000 miles above the equator. Together, their cameras can photograph the entire earth, except the poles. Other satellites follow north-south and south-north routes from pole to pole.

Weather balloon

4 The long tails of weather balloons are equipped with radiosondes. These are radio transmitters that measure temperature, air pressure, and humidity in the atmosphere. Some balloons ascend as high as 90,000 feet to collect data.

5 Weather monitoring equipment is attached to airplanes. These planes can fly directly into storms to take measurements.

6 About 10,000 weather stations around the world send reports every three hours to 13 weather centers operated by the World Meteorological Organization.

Weather vane

7 Probably the most familiar piece of weather equipment is the weather vane. It's certainly one of the oldest. Weather vanes have been around since the ninth century. They indicate the direction the wind is blowing.

8 Radar equipment sends signals into clouds. These signals are then converted into images on radar screens, allowing meteorologists to track storms.

9 Other stations drift at sea and transmit data to satellites.

Adapted from *Kids Discover*.

Before you read

Look at the pictures on the opposite page. Then check (✔) what you think the text will be about.

_____ 1. the different weather-monitoring equipment that meteorologists use to make forecasts

_____ 2. the reasons it is difficult for meteorologists to forecast the weather

_____ 3. the differences between instruments meteorologists used to forecast the weather 50 years ago and the instruments they use today

_____ 4. the reasons it is important for meteorologists to collect data from all over the globe

Reading

Scan the text to check your predictions. Then read the whole text.

After you read

A **Find the words in _italics_ in the reading. Then match each word with its meaning.**

_e_	1. _orbit_ (par. 1)	a. change something into a different form
___	2. _ascend_ (par. 4)	b. move slowly with no control over direction
___	3. _convert_ (par. 8)	c. send
___	4. _track_ (par. 8)	d. go up
___	5. _drift_ (par. 9)	e. move in a curved path, for example, around Earth
___	6. _transmit_ (par. 9)	f. follow the movement of something, for example, with radar

B **Write the number of the paragraph where each sentence could go.**

_7_ a. You can see them on the roofs of many houses around the world.

___ b. It is very dangerous but important work.

___ c. They take photos of the North and South Poles.

___ d. These stations on the ocean send information about weather conditions.

___ e. They can't usually measure the speed of the wind, however.

___ f. This is located in Geneva, Switzerland.

C **Answer these questions.**

1. Based only on the weather, where in the world would you most like to live? Where would you not like to live?

2. People in some lines of work need to pay close attention to weather forecasts. What are some examples of occupations where the weather is particularly important? Why is the weather so important for them?

3. In the United States, people say that when pine cones close up, rain is coming. What are some other non-technological ways of predicting the weather?

Nature's weather forecasters

1   When people want to find out about the weather, they usually go to their radios, TVs, newspapers, or to the Internet. However, you can also find many weather signs among wildlife, because of their highly developed senses. Drops in air pressure affect small mammals and insects in many ways. Try looking in or near the house. Mice and cockroaches are good weather indicators. People who spend a lot of time outdoors have observed that field mice come out of their holes, squeak, and run around before a storm. Cockroaches become more active before a storm too.

2   Deer leave the high ground and come down from the mountains before a storm. If you see this, you can be sure that there will be a storm within two days.

3   When you see large numbers of sea crabs on a sandy beach, it is time to leave. A change in air pressure over the water warns the crabs that a storm is coming. To escape the stormy sea pounding the shore, they leave the water and seek shelter on land.

4   Birds are especially good weather indicators because they also show the effect of a pressure drop in many ways. For example, some birds become irritable and quarrelsome and will fight over a piece of bread. Other birds chirp and sing just before a storm. It seems they know they won't get another chance for an hour or two. Birds also seek shelter before a storm. You will sometimes see birds roosting in trees or huddling together on a wire close to a building. This is a good storm signal. Pre-storm low pressure makes the air so thin that birds have difficulty flying, so they go to roost.

5   Seabirds sit out a storm on land. Anytime you see seagulls or other seabirds sitting on the ground in large groups, reluctant to fly, it is not a very good day to go sailing.

6   It is unusual to see large flocks of birds flying overhead in the summertime, rather than during the periods of migration in the spring or fall. Watch for other weather signs if you see this. You should also stay alert if you see migrating birds flying in the wrong direction. These birds may be flying ahead of a storm.

7   And if you can't see a bird anywhere, look out! They may have flown to a different place because a violent storm was coming in their direction.

8   By paying closer attention to some important clues in nature, we can become better prepared for any kind of weather.

READING TIP
Sometimes words that are close in meaning appear together or nearby. For example, *irritable* and *quarrelsome* are similar in meaning. This is also true about *chirp* and *sing* and *roosting* and *huddling*.

Adapted from *Nature's Weather Forecasters*.

Before you read

Using previous knowledge

What happens to wildlife before a storm? Circle the information you think is correct.

1. Mice **come out of** / **stay in** their holes.
2. Cockroaches become **more** / **less** active.
3. Deer **stay up in** / **come down from** the mountains.
4. Crabs **stay in the water** / **come onto land**.
5. Seagulls **sit on the ground** / **fly around**.
6. Birds fly **in large flocks** / **separately**.
7. Birds make **more** / **less** noise.

Reading

Scanning

Scan the text to check your answers. Then read the whole text.

After you read

Guessing meaning from context

A **Find the words in *italics* in the reading. Then complete the sentences.**

active (par. 1)   *quarrelsome* (par. 4)   *reluctant* (par. 5)
seek shelter (par. 3)   *roost* (par. 4)   *migrate* (par. 6)

1. When birds ___migrate___, they move from one part of the country or part of the world to another.
2. When you are _____ to do something, you do not want to do it, try not to do it, or do it more slowly.
3. When people are _____, they fight a lot with others.
4. When people are _____, they behave in a lively, busy way.
5. When animals _____, they look for a place to protect themselves from the weather.
6. When birds _____, they rest or sleep in a particular place.

Understanding details

B **Mark each sentence true (*T*), false (*F*), or does not give the information (*?*).**

___T___ 1. Lower air pressure affects wildlife.

_____ 2. Lower air temperature affects wildlife.

_____ 3. Other animals besides deer come down from the mountains before a storm.

_____ 4. All animals seek shelter before a storm.

_____ 5. Birds show that a storm is coming in different ways.

Relating reading to personal experience

C **Answer these questions.**

1. Which animal behavior could you most easily observe near your home? Have you ever seen such behavior?
2. Which other wild animals do you know of that behave differently before a storm?
3. Do you notice that your own behavior changes before a storm? If so, how?

Could you survive a natural disaster?

Most people do not like to think about disasters, so they do not prepare for them. This is a deadly mistake. Your survival depends on preparation. Here are some tips that could save your life.

1

- Choose an out-of-town person each family member can call after the disaster if you become separated. In addition, choose two nearby places where family members know to meet. One should be close to your home. The other should be outside your neighborhood, in case floods or fires keep you away from your home.

- Keep your important papers in a safety-deposit box at the bank or another safe place.

- Leave a disaster-supply kit (see section 5) in a closet near the front door. Make sure you keep the kit filled with fresh food and water.

- If you are advised to evacuate, leave the area right away.

2

You may have some time to prepare before certain types of disasters such as hurricanes, tornadoes, and floods.

- Bring in garbage cans, lawn furniture, and bicycles — anything that could fly around or blow away.

- Fill your gas tank, and prepare your car for evacuation.

- Fill bottles, jugs, and even bathtubs with drinking water.

- During floods, move your possessions to higher floors.

- Keep your radio on for weather information.

3

Hurricane or flood: Stay in an interior space with no windows. Glass could break and hurt you.

Earthquake: Get under the nearest heavy desk or table. This will protect you from falling objects such as books.

Tornado: Go to the lowest place possible, such as a basement, to be safe from flying objects. If you don't have a basement, go to an interior space with no windows, such as a bathroom or a closet.

4

Hurricane or flood
- During hurricane season, keep a two-week supply of prescription drugs.
- Have wood and nails ready to board up windows.

Earthquake
- Move beds away from windows, heavy pictures, or mirrors.
- Place large and/or heavy objects on lower shelves
- Learn how to shut off the electricity, gas, and water.

Tornado
- Pick one place in the home where family members will gather together when there is a tornado warning.

5 *Your disaster-supply kit*
First-aid kit and prescriptions
Canned food and can opener
Bottled water
Extra clothes and blankets
Battery-operated radio
Flashlight and extra batteries
Car keys
Cash and credit card
Important phone numbers

Adapted from *McCall's Magazine.*

Before you read

These headings are missing from the boxes on the opposite page. Write three pieces of advice you think you will read in the text.

Your disaster-supply kit
The safest places
Preparing for the worst—do this now!

_____

_____

_____

Reading

Scan the text to check your predictions. Then read the whole text.

After you read

A **For which boxes in the text are these good headings? Write the numbers.**

   _5_   a. Your disaster-supply kit

   _____   b. The safest places

   _____   c. Preparing for the worst—do this now!

   _____   d. The disaster-ready home

   _____   e. Getting through the first hour

B **Which natural disasters are the people following advice for? Write _hurricane_, _tornado_, _flood_, _earthquake_, or _all disasters_.**

1. _____tornado_____   2. _____   3. _____   4. _____

5. _____   6. _____   7. _____   8. _____

C **Answer these questions.**

1. Which of the advice in the reading do you already follow? Which of the advice do you think is not very useful?

2. What things in your home could be dangerous during a natural disaster?

3. What other natural disasters can you think of? How can you prepare for them?

Vocabulary expansion

A Complete the chart with the missing words.

	Adjective	Noun	Verb
1.	active	action	*act*
2.	convertible	conversion	
3.	equipped	equipment	
4.		humidity	humidify
5.	migratory		migrate
6.	predictable	prediction	
7.	quarrelsome		quarrel
8.		storm	storm

B Read the sentences. Write the parts of speech of the missing words. Then complete the sentences with the correct words from the chart.

1. A volcano that is ____active____ is one that might still erupt sometime.
      adj.

2. I don't like _____ weather. All the wind and rain makes me feel sad.

3. Weather forecasters use a lot of different _____ to make forecasts.

4. To understand the temperature in another country, people may have to _____ Celsius into Fahrenheit.

5. _____ birds are often seen flying over the area in large numbers.

6. It's easier to _____ tomorrow's weather than the weather five days from now.

7. I don't mind hot weather; it's the _____ I can't stand.

The weather and you

You are going to interview another student and find out how the weather affects him or her. Read the questions, and add two more questions to ask. Then report your partner's answers to the rest of the class.

1. How do you usually find out about the current weather? Where do you get the forecast for the coming days?
2. How often do you talk to friends, neighbors, or family about the weather?
3. How does weather affect your mood? How do you feel on sunny or rainy days?
4. _____
5. _____

UNIT

6 Clothes

You are going to read three texts about clothes. First, answer the questions in the boxes.

Dressing for success

This magazine article describes what you should wear to a job interview and the effect of clothing on getting a job.

1. What do a person's clothes tell you about that person?
2. What do you think a young person should wear to a job interview? Why?

Casual dress in the workplace

Should people be allowed to dress casually at work? Find out about the trend toward casual dress at work and what people think about it.

1. What types of workers can dress casually at work? Why?
2. For which jobs do people have to wear suits or conservative clothes? What image do conservative clothes give?

T-shirts out; uniforms in

This newspaper article outlines some of the benefits of school uniforms.

1. Did/do you wear a uniform in school? Why do you think school uniforms are used around the world?
2. Which professions require employees to wear uniforms at work? Why do you think they have to wear uniforms?

Vocabulary

Find out the meanings of the words in *italics*. Then answer the questions about the people in the picture.

1. Which people are wearing *casual* clothes?
2. Which person is wearing the most *conservative* clothes?
3. Which person is wearing the most *stylish* clothes?
4. Which people are wearing an *outfit*?
5. Which person is most interested in *fashion*?
6. Which person is the most *dressed up*?
7. Which person *dresses* most like you?

Alison   David   Serena   Rick

Dressing *for* success

1 Sandra, a college senior, learned a painful lesson in how to dress for success at a recent job information session at her college. The employer was a computer company. The dress code was "stylishly casual," so Sandra wasn't worried about going to the meeting right after class. After all, she was wearing a new pair of denim bell-bottom trousers and a black fur-collared coat. That was a big mistake. Almost everyone else at the meeting was wearing conservative outfits; and as soon as she walked in, she knew she was dressed inappropriately. For much of the session, the presenters stared at her. In the end, she did not get a job offer.

2 While denim may be fine at most restaurants or at a concert, there are at least three activities that still call for a suit: weddings, funerals, and job interviews. This may come as a surprise to many graduates, says Marilyn Santiesteban. Her company runs courses that teach people what to wear and how to present themselves. Despite the fact that "our society has changed, and there are no more rules, the expectations are still there," she says.

3 Dressing conservatively shows that you are serious about the meeting and interested in the job, says Richard Wonder. He specializes in getting people technology jobs. "A suit gives the impression that the interviewee will conform to company policies and be a team player."

4 David Lo's strategy can benefit other job seekers. Lo, a graduate student, prepares carefully for an interview. First, he tries to find out as much as he can about the company. Then he chooses his shirts and ties accordingly. "For IBM, I dressed very conservatively: white shirt, striped tie, black shoes. But for Andersen Consulting, I wore an indigo shirt and a purple striped tie. It differs based on what I think they are expecting and the company's reputation." Lo's is a smart strategy because companies want to hire employees who are "their kind of people."

Adapted from *Computerworld*.

Before you read

Look at the title and the pictures on the opposite page. Match the descriptions with the correct picture. Then answer the question in the box.

Thinking about personal experience

1. bell-bottom trousers and a fur-collared coat
2. a suit and a striped tie

Who is wearing appropriate clothes for a job interview?

Reading

Scanning

Scan the text to check your answer. Then read the whole text.

After you read

Guessing meaning from context

A Find the words in *italics* in the reading. Then match each word with its meaning. (Be careful! There is one extra answer.)

_d_	1. *painful* (par. 1)	a. behave in the same way as the group
	2. *stare* (par. 1)	b. sick
	3. *call for* (par. 2)	c. a plan for achieving a goal
	4. *conform* (par. 3)	d. difficult
	5. *benefit* (par. 4)	e. in a way that is correct for the situation
	6. *strategy* (par. 4)	f. look at directly for a long time
	7. *accordingly* (par. 4)	g. require
		h. be helpful to

Understanding details

B Mark each sentence true (*T*), false (*F*), or does not give the information (*?*).

_F_ 1. Sandra got a job offer after the job interview session.

_____ 2. Everyone at the job information session got a job except Sandra.

_____ 3. People in the computer business always wear casual clothes.

_____ 4. College students who want to get a job after graduation should get a suit.

_____ 5. During an interview, people judge you by what you are wearing.

_____ 6. All companies have a similar dress code.

_____ 7. David Lo got a job.

Relating reading to personal experience

C Answer these questions.

1. When Sandra realized her mistake, do you think she should have apologized and explained what had happened? Why or why not?
2. How can a suit show that someone "will conform to company policies and be a team player"?
3. Have you ever had a job interview? If so, what did you wear? Did you get the job?

Casual dress in the workplace

1 For Ruth Russell, Friday isn't just another workday. It's the one day she can wear a sweater and casual slacks instead of a business suit. An employee at an insurance company, Russell loves the day away from her usual dressy suits and high-heeled shoes: "It's a real treat. It puts us in a good mood and winds the week down." Russell has joined thousands of workers across the United States who happily change from jackets, ties, and dresses to jeans, polo shirts, and sweaters on Fridays.

2 Why dress-down Friday? "I think it gives an atmosphere of less formality," says President Matthew Augustine of Eltrex Industries. Today, dressing casually on the job is a way to show your company is in style. Another contributor is faxes, voice mail, and e-mail, which have reduced public contact. With fewer out-of-the-office meetings, people are dressing less to impress and more for comfort, experts say.

3 However, even though dressing down is popular, the trend is controversial. Some workers remain strongly opposed. "You've got all the time in the world to dress down when you retire," declared one woman. Others worry that dressing casually — even for one day — lowers an employer's professional image. "We had some very important clients come in on a Friday a few months ago," says another worker. "These people dressed in navy suits. Our people dressed way down. I thought it was

embarrassing. It sent the wrong message about our company." Many people feel that suits, ties, and dresses are superior to casual clothes in creating a positive professional image.

4 Will the dress-down trend last? Some experts think it will go away one day. As long as the trend continues, though, dressing casually can cause a little confusion in the workplace. Businesspeople aren't sure what to wear, and many people just put on whatever they feel like in the morning. The casual-dress trend worries Elizabeth Csordas, director of the fashion program at Marist College. She believes dressing down at work is one of the signs that society is lowering its standards in everything. Csordas and John T. Malloy, author of *Dress for Success*, say psychological changes occur when people dress up. "There's no question what you wear affects what you do, your performance, and your attitude," says Malloy.

Adapted from *Gannett News Service*.

Before you read

Look at these sentences from the text. Then check (✔) the statement below that you think best describes what the text will be about.

Why dress-down Friday?
However, even though dressing down is popular, the trend is controversial.
Will the dress-down trend last?

_____ 1. In the past, office workers wore suits, dresses, or skirts. Now they wear casual clothes to work every day. Not everybody is happy about this change.

_____ 2. Some companies allow workers to wear casual clothes on Fridays. Both workers and bosses are happy about this change.

_____ 3. Some companies allow workers to wear casual clothes on Fridays. Not everybody is happy about this change.

Reading

Scan the text to check your prediction. Then read the whole text.

After you read

A **Find the words in *italics* in the reading. Then complete the sentences.**

formality (par. 2)   *atmosphere* (par. 2)   *impress* (par. 2)   *retire* (par. 3)   *embarrassing* (par. 3)

1. The __atmosphere__ at the office is very friendly. It's a nice place to work.

2. I was the only one at the party who wasn't dressed up. It was very _____.

3. When I'm 65 years old and I _____, I'm going to have a lot of free time.

4. I don't like the _____ of the company. We have to wear suits every day.

5. I want people to have a good opinion of me. I want to _____ people.

B **Check (✔) the correct column.**

	Reasons for casual clothes	Reasons against casual clothes
1. It puts workers in a good mood.	✔	
2. There are fewer out-of-the-office meetings.		
3. It lowers an employer's professional image.		
4. There will be time to dress down after retirement.		
5. It can cause confusion in the workplace.		

C **Answer these questions.**

1. Do you think casual dress is suitable for the workplace? Why or why not?
2. Imagine you have a job and are allowed to dress down at work. What do you wear?
3. Do you think that what you wear affects your job performance? Why or why not?

T-shirts out; uniforms in

1 School uniforms are becoming more and more popular across the U.S.A. That's no surprise, because they offer many benefits. They instantly end the powerful social sorting and labeling that come from clothing. If all students are dressed in the same way, they will not be distracted by fashion competition. Some students will also not be excluded or laughed at because they wear the "wrong" clothes.

2 Some people object to the "regimentation" of school uniforms, but they do not realize that students already accept a kind of regimentation — wanting to look just like their friends. The difference is that the clothing students choose for themselves creates social barriers; school uniforms tear those barriers down.

3 As in other places, uniforms remind the wearers of their purpose and responsibilities. When a man or woman puts on a police uniform, for example, he or she becomes, for a time, the symbol of law and order. The

uniform signifies to the wearer his or her special duties and sends the same message to everyone the wearer meets. Many different professions wear uniforms of one kind or another. For students, the school uniform reminds them that their responsibility for the six or seven hours they are in school is to get an education.

4 Some parents complain that school uniforms will affect their children's "creativity." First, as

noted above, the clothes students typically wear do not express their individuality. They just copy their classmates. Second, students have the rest of the day to be as creative as they like.

While they're in school, their job is to master reading, writing, and arithmetic; this should engage all the creativity they have. Mastery of those skills will enrich the creativity the students apply in every aspect of their lives.

Adapted from *The Columbus Dispatch*.

READING TIP
When you want to understand the main points, skim the text first. Read through it quickly, without looking for details.

Before you read

Check (✔) the statements you agree with.

	Me	Writer
1. There are many advantages to school uniforms.		
2. The clothes young people wear express their creativity.		
3. School uniforms help students concentrate on their schoolwork.		
4. Students should be allowed to wear whatever they want to school.		

Reading

Skim the text and check (✔) the statements in the chart above that the writer agrees with. Then read the whole text.

After you read

A **Circle the correct answers.**

1. When you *sort* things, you separate them into groups. *Social sorting* (par. 1) probably means
   a. separating people into groups.
   b. separating clothes into groups.
2. When there is *competition*, people try to do better than others. *Fashion competition* (par. 1) probably means
   a. having a fashion show.
   b. trying to have the nicest clothes.
3. *Regimentation* is extreme organization and control of people. *Regimentation of school uniforms* (par. 2) probably means
   a. parents' control of their children's clothes.
   b. wearing only certain clothes.
4. *Barriers* stop people from doing something. *Social barriers* (par. 2) probably means
   a. stopping people from being friends with everybody.
   b. stopping people from wearing what they want.

B **Match each paragraph with its main idea. (Be careful! There are two extra answers.)**

_f_	1. Paragraph 1	a. There are reasons why people have to wear uniforms.
	2. Paragraph 2	b. School uniforms do not affect students' creativity.
	3. Paragraph 3	c. Uniforms are good for some students.
	4. Paragraph 4	d. Students try to look like each other, and this causes problems.
		e. Some parents think uniforms are a good idea.
		f. Uniforms are good for all students.

C **Answer these questions.**

1. Do you think school uniforms are a good or bad idea? Why?
2. Do you think people's clothes show their creativity? Why or why not?
3. Imagine someone asks you to design a better school uniform. What does it look like?

Vocabulary expansion

A Write the letter(s) of the sentences that describe each picture.

1. _a, b, d_

2. _____

3. _____ *Swimming practice starts in five minutes.*

4. _____

5. _____

a. He is *wearing* glasses.
b. He *has* a jacket on.
c. He's *getting undressed.*
d. He's *trying on* a jacket.
e. He was *dressed up.*

f. She's *putting on* her shoes.
g. She's going to *change.*
h. She's *getting dressed.*
i. She's *taking off* her earrings.
j. She *puts on* a bathing suit when she goes to the pool.

B Answer these questions.

1. What time did you get dressed today?
2. What do you like to wear to class?
3. When you came into the classroom today, did you take off anything?
4. When you leave class today, are you going to put on anything?
5. What do you have on today?
6. Is anyone in the class dressed up today? If so, who?
7. When you get home today, are you going to change?
8. Do you usually try on clothes before you buy them?

Clothes and you

Take part in a fashion show! Work in pairs. First, take detailed notes on what your partner is wearing. Then describe these clothes as he or she walks down the "runway" in the class's fashion show.

UNIT 7 Culture

You are going to read three texts about culture. First, answer the questions in the boxes.

READING 1

Adventures in India

Read diary entries from the website of someone who spent a year in India on a student exchange program.

1. How do you think life in your country is different from life in India?
2. What would be good and bad about living in a different country for a year?

READING 2

Body language in the United States

How do Americans greet each other? How close to each other do they stand in public? Read this excerpt from a book to find out.

1. How do people in your country greet each other? Do they ever shake hands? Do they ever kiss or hug?
2. When people in your country stand and talk, how close do they stand to each other?

READING 3

Cross-cultural differences

What happens when people from different cultures meet? Read this excerpt from a journal and learn what one British writer thinks.

1. Is it easy to get along with people from different cultures? Why or why not?
2. Do you like being with people from different cultures, or does this make you feel uncomfortable? Why?

Vocabulary

Find out the meanings of the words in the box. Mark each one positive in meaning (+), negative in meaning (-), or neutral (✔).

accustomed	lack of interest	relationship building
bewildered	misunderstandings	to respect
different values	mutual trust	rudeness

Adventures in India

1 *I have spent a year in India on a student exchange program. These diary entries deal with the good and bad times I have been through there. They will give you an idea of what it is like to live in this country.*

January 10

2 We got on the train, slept, read, talked, ate, watched the countryside, and before I had realized what was happening, the 27 hours of journey were behind us, and we had arrived in Delhi.

3 I really enjoyed that journey. We had a compartment nearly to ourselves. I slept surprisingly well, despite the noise — I guess the train rocked me to sleep. The only problem was my painful stomachache.

March 12

4 I am suddenly overcome by the feeling that I am alone in this unknown town. The stress of the last weeks has been gently adding up, and I am feeling quite miserable. I met a Japanese student from England, and it is a great relief to be able to share my feelings with somebody who has lived in the same world as me. Of course, my Indian friends are very understanding, but I guess that you cannot really understand how distressing India can be for a foreigner if you are not a foreigner yourself.

June 23

5 The monsoon seems to have started. We have had occasional rain these last weeks, but for the past couple of days, we have been waking up to find our garden flooded. All this rain brings me back to my arrival here and the terror that I felt.

September 9

6 A new group of students arrived today. Seeing them all clean, fresh, and bewildered reminds me of my arrival in India so many months ago. I suddenly realize how much I have learned and how accustomed I am to this new country. I am no longer lost and ignorant. I know my way through town, public transportation, hotels and restaurants. It is quite a good feeling to be the one "who knows" — even though I don't know *that* much.

November 18

7 The last weeks have run by like goats on the street. I have only a month left in this country, so much to do, and so little time. My room is filled with things to pack, and my head is trying to summarize my "Indian experience." As days go by, I try to fix in my memory all the things that I will soon forget. Small, daily, unimportant events that would have seemed incredible a year ago.

December 15

8 As my departure gets closer, I'm tired and looking forward to going home. I want to see my country and family again — although I dread leaving India. It's not like the homesickness I was feeling last winter. Now I wish I could take India back home with me.

Adapted from *www.climbtothestars.org/india/*

Before you read

Imagine that you go to another country for a year. Check (✔) the feelings you may have.

_____	1. loneliness	_____	5. misery
_____	2. bewilderment	_____	6. terror
_____	3. happiness	_____	7. homesickness
_____	4. confusion	_____	8. ignorance

Reading

Scan the text to find the writer's feelings. Then read the whole text.

After you read

A | **Circle the main idea of each diary entry.**

1. January 10
   ⓐ the train ride to Delhi
   b. the arrival in India

2. March 12
   a. the need to meet people who understand you
   b. the living conditions in India

3. June 23
   a. feelings of homesickness
   b. the weather

4. September 9
   a. better feelings about living in India
   b. friendships with new students

5. November 18
   a. so many things to pack
   b. getting ready to leave

6. December 15
   a. excitement about going home
   b. mixed feelings about leaving India

B | **Check (✔) the correct column.**

The writer's feelings	Positive	Negative	Positive & negative
1. during the train ride to Delhi	✓		
2. after about eight weeks in India			
3. after about eight months in India			
4. a month before she left India			
5. days before she left India			
6. about her year in India			

C | **Answer these questions.**

1. Would you like to go to another country on a student exchange program? Why or why not?

2. If you could go to another country for a period of time, which country would you choose? Why? How do you think life there is different from life in your country?

3. What do you think exchange students who are visiting your country find interesting and/or different?

Body language in the United States

Here are some things you might notice on a visit to the United States.

1 Most people use a firm handshake, accompanied by direct eye contact, as the standard greeting. Occasionally, among very good friends, women may briefly hug other women, and men may quickly kiss the cheek of a woman. Males rarely hug one another, however. Occasionally, men may shake hands with the left hand either covering the handshake or lightly gripping the forearm. This shows greater warmth and friendship.

2 Many people in the United States tend to stand just about one arm's length away from each other while talking or standing in public. This is called "the comfort zone."

3 Many American women still enjoy having men open doors for them, help them get seated, and give up their seats in public transportation. With increasing emphasis on equality between the sexes, however, there are some women who object to this type of behavior.

4 To call or ask someone to come over, people usually raise an index finger and then bend and straighten it, or raise the hand (palm facing inward) and curl the fingers quickly towards him or herself. Either is acceptable. To call a waiter, they generally just raise one index finger to head level or above.

5 Americans consider direct eye contact very important in both social and business situations. Failure to make and maintain eye contact implies boredom or lack of interest.

6 People in the United States generally respect lines in public situations and form lines in an orderly fashion. Shoving or pushing one's way into such a line will probably cause both anger and complaints.

7 Most people wave "hello" or "goodbye" by extending the arm, palm facing outward, and twisting the hand at the wrist. Another way is to raise the arm, palm outward, and move the whole arm and hand back and forth. This may be important to know because in many other countries this is a signal for "no."

8 Americans quickly try to make conversation if silence occurs during business or social situations. Many Americans become uncomfortable with periods of silence.

9 It is common and acceptable for people to use the hand and index finger to point at objects or to indicate directions.

10 American mothers sometimes scold children by shaking an index finger at them. People admire children by patting them on the top of the head.

> **READING TIP**
> The same word in English can have different meanings, depending on its part of speech. For example, *object* in "women who object to this" (par. 3) means "dislike." *Object* in "point at objects" (par. 9) means "a thing."

Adapted from *Gestures: The Do's and Taboos of Body Language Around the World.*

Before you read

Look at the pictures. Then check (✔) the gestures that are common in your country, and write what they mean.

1. 2. 3. 4. 5.

Reading

Scan the text to find the meanings of the gestures above in the United States. Match each gesture with one of these sentences. Then read the whole text.

  _5_   a. "You're a nice little girl."   _____ d. "It's over there."

  _____ b. "Hi. It's nice to see you."   _____ e. "Come here, please."

  _____ c. "Goodbye."

After you read

A **Find the words in *italics* in the reading. Then match each word with its meaning.**

  _e_   1. *grip* (par. 1)   a. push away

  _____ 2. *imply* (par. 5)   b. move the hand

  _____ 3. *shove* (par. 6)   c. touch lightly

  _____ 4. *wave* (par. 7)   d. mean

  _____ 5. *extend* (par. 7)   e. hold tightly

  _____ 6. *pat* (par. 10)   f. stretch

B **Check (✔) the statements that describe acceptable behavior in the United States.**

  _✔_   1. Men shake hands with their left hands covering the handshake.

  _____ 2. Two businessmen speak while standing closer than an arm's length apart.

  _____ 3. A man does not make eye contact with a woman during a business meeting.

  _____ 4. A young woman with a baby tries to push her way into a line of people.

  _____ 5. A mother shakes her index finger at her young child.

C **Answer these questions.**

1. Which information in the reading is true about your country? Which is not true?
2. What five things should foreign visitors know about acceptable and unacceptable behavior in your country?
3. How would you react if you saw a visitor to your country using unacceptable body language? Give some examples.

Cross-cultural differences

A British perspective

1 Encountering people from another culture can be difficult at the very least. From the beginning, people may send the wrong signal. Or they may ignore signals from another person who is trying to develop the relationship.

2 Different cultures place varying amounts of emphasis on the importance of relationship building. For example, business in Turkey is not possible until there is a relationship of mutual trust. Even with people at work, it is necessary for people to spend a lot of time in "small talk," usually over a glass of tea, before they do any job. Haste equals rudeness.

3 In many European countries, too — like the UK, France, or Spain — people find it easier to build up a working relationship in social settings. It is at restaurants or cafés, and not at the office, where people form lasting working relationships.

4 Talk and silence may also vary in some cultures. I once made a presentation in Bangkok to local staff. I was sure it was going to be a success, but for some reason it was not. The staff stared at me blankly and smiled. My presentation began to fall apart. Nobody asked any questions. I had expected my presentation to start a lively discussion; instead there was an uncomfortable silence.

5 After getting to know Thai ways better, I realized that the staff thought I was talking too much. In my own culture, we express meaning mainly through words. We speak a great deal to express what we feel and think, and silence makes us uncomfortable. In some other cultures, people understand a lot of what is happening from the context, and sometimes feel too many words are unnecessary. People communicate in an unspoken way.

6 Even within Northern Europe, cross-cultural differences can cause misunderstandings. Certainly, English and German cultures share similar values; however, Germans tend to get down to business more quickly. Typical British comments of our neighbors include such descriptions as "overbearing" and "rude." In fact, this is just because one culture starts discussions and makes decisions more quickly.

7 People from different parts of the world have different values, and sometimes these values clash head-on. Nevertheless, if we can understand and appreciate these differences, a multicultural environment can be a wonderful learning opportunity.

Adapted from *The Organisation*.

Before you read

Check (✔) the business customs you think are generally true.

_____ 1. In business, a relationship of mutual trust is important.   _____

_____ 2. "Small talk," or social conversation, is important at work.   _____

_____ 3. Haste, or doing something in a hurry, is considered rude.   _____

_____ 4. People build up working relationships in social settings.   _____

_____ 5. People speak a great deal to express what they feel and think.   _____

_____ 6. Working people usually get down to business quickly.   _____

Reading

Scan the text to find out where the sentences above are true. Write the names of the countries next to the sentences. Then read the whole text.

After you read

A **Who do you think the text was written for? Check (✔) the correct answer.**

_____ 1. people who want to learn about British culture

_____ 2. people who travel to different countries because of their jobs

_____ 3. college students who are taking a foreign language course

B **Find the words or phrases in *italics* in the reading. Circle the meaning of each word or phrase.**

1. When you *encounter* someone, you (meet them for the first time)/ know them for a long time. (par. 1)
2. When you *send the wrong signal*, you **help people understand what you mean** / **do something that confuses people.** (par. 1)
3. When things *vary*, they are **the same** / **different.** (par. 4)
4. When you *stare at people blankly*, you **look at them as if you don't see them** / **look at them with understanding.** (par. 4)
5. When people are *overbearing*, they **ask you for help** / **tell you what to do.** (par. 6)
6. When ideas *clash head-on*, they are **completely different** / **exactly the same.** (par. 7)
7. When you *appreciate* something, you **talk about it** / **feel it is important.** (par. 7)

C **Answer these questions.**

1. In what ways is your culture similar to and different from the cultures of the countries mentioned in the text?
2. What values are important in your country? Do you think other cultures share these same values?
3. Do you think it is important for people to understand how cultures around the world are different? Why or why not?

Vocabulary expansion

A Add the prefixes *un-* or *in-* to change the meanings of the words below.

1. *un* able	5. ___complete	9. ___expensive	13. ___known
2. ___acceptable	6. ___convenient	10. ___formal	14. ___necessary
3. ___aware	7. ___correct	11. ___friendly	15. ___spoken
4. ___comfortable	8. ___credible	12. ___important	16. ___successful

B Read the story. Then complete the sentences with words from exercise A.

I wanted to get to know my new neighbors because I didn't want them to think I was
____unfriendly____. They were from another country that I thought I knew well. In the end,
however, my knowledge of their culture was _____. First of all, I remembered
reading somewhere that people give welcome gifts, so I bought my neighbors something
nice but _____. This was a big mistake. I was _____ that it is
_____ for strangers to buy welcome gifts. Only family members give them,
and these gifts always cost a lot of money. Then I invited the neighbors to my home for
coffee in the afternoon. This was _____ for them, since the whole family usually
ate together at this time. When I invited them to sit in my kitchen, I could see that they
were_____; but I didn't know why. I later learned that in their culture it is too
_____ to have guests sit in the kitchen. They always sit in the living room.
Finally, since they didn't speak my language, and I didn't speak theirs, we were
_____ to communicate.

Culture and you

A stereotype is an idea that many people believe to be true about another group of people.
While this idea may apply to some individuals, it is not necessarily true of the entire group.

1. Work in pairs. Discuss the parts of this description that you think are stereotypes.

> Americans live in big cities. They all drive, and they drive big cars. They
> are very religious. They carry guns. They eat hamburgers all the time.

2. Now, with your partner, make a list of the stereotypes you think foreigners have about
   people from your country. Compare your list with another pair.

UNIT 8 Outer space

You are going to read three texts about outer space. First, answer the questions in the boxes.

READING 1

Living in space

What is it like to live in zero gravity in outer space? Find out about some aspects of life aboard a spacecraft.

1. How do astronauts and cosmonauts spend their time in space?
2. Think of some routine activities people do every day. How are these activities different in space?

READING 2

SUN

MARS
EARTH
VENUS   JUPITER
MERCURY

The planets

How much do you know about the planets in our solar system? Check your knowledge about the planetary system in this reading.

1. How many of the planets can you name in English?
2. What do you know about each of the planets?

READING 3

Space tours not so far off

Would you like to take a trip to outer space? Read this newspaper article to find out when this may be possible.

1. Would you like to take a trip to outer space? Why or why not?
2. When do you think it will be possible for the average person to travel to outer space?

Vocabulary
Find out the meanings of the words in *italics*.

1. People and things *float* in space because they are *weightless*.
2. The *solar system* is the sun and all the planets, comets, and *asteroids* that go around it.
3. The planets *orbit* the sun.
4. A planet's *atmosphere* is the layer of air or other gas around it.
5. Scientists want to have a *space station* so that they can do research about space.
6. There is no water on the *surface* of the moon.

Living in space

1   What would life be like aboard a spacecraft? Perhaps the strangest and most interesting feature about living in space is that people are weightless because there is no gravity. This condition, which is called zero gravity, makes it possible for astronauts to fly through the cabin simply by pushing off from a wall or chair. It's almost like swimming underwater, except that there is no up or down.

2   Imagine, then, taking a shower when water floats in the air instead of flowing down on you. Or strapping yourself to a wall so you don't float away while taking a nap. You couldn't brush your teeth in the usual way. Read the following to understand how these and other routine activities can be major tasks for people who travel in space.

Showers

3   Taking a shower aboard a spacecraft isn't like taking one at home. On a spacecraft, you must conserve water, and preparing the equipment for showers takes a long time. It is also a complicated activity. On Russian spacecrafts, a cosmonaut gets in an elastic cylinder with caps at both ends. Rubber slippers, fastened to the floor, keep the cosmonaut from floating upward. The cosmonaut inserts a flexible hose into his or her mouth in order to breathe. Then the cosmonaut puts a clip on his or her nose to keep water out, because water doesn't flow downward in space. When the water is turned on, it comes out of holes at the top and bottom of the cylinder. Cosmonauts use a soap-filled cloth to wash, and then a plain cloth to rinse.

Teeth cleaning

4   Astronauts and cosmonauts use electric toothbrushes. They are encouraged to massage their gums with a special tissue or cloth. A special chewing gum, used after every meal, also helps them keep their teeth clean.

Sleep

5   When you're really tired, it feels wonderful to lie down on a bed and sleep. In space, however, there is no "down." An astronaut sleeps in a standing position in a sleeping bag attached to the wall of a sleeping compartment. In the space station *Freedom*, elastic bands keep the sleeper in place and give the feeling of lying horizontally on a bed. These bands press the sleeper back in the same way that gravity presses down.

Adapted from *Living in Space.*

Before you read

Check (✔) the pictures that show what you think life is like aboard a spacecraft.

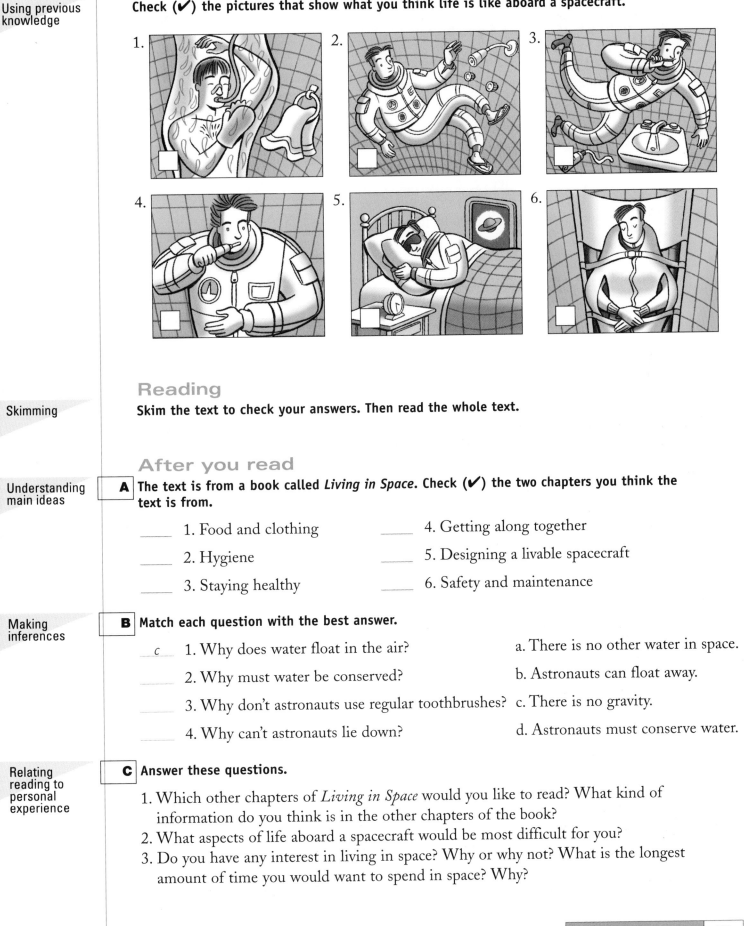

1.   2.   3.

4.   5.   6.

Reading

Skim the text to check your answers. Then read the whole text.

After you read

A The text is from a book called *Living in Space*. Check (✔) the two chapters you think the text is from.

_____ 1. Food and clothing   _____ 4. Getting along together

_____ 2. Hygiene   _____ 5. Designing a livable spacecraft

_____ 3. Staying healthy   _____ 6. Safety and maintenance

B Match each question with the best answer.

_c_ 1. Why does water float in the air?   a. There is no other water in space.

_____ 2. Why must water be conserved?   b. Astronauts can float away.

_____ 3. Why don't astronauts use regular toothbrushes? c. There is no gravity.

_____ 4. Why can't astronauts lie down?   d. Astronauts must conserve water.

C Answer these questions.

1. Which other chapters of *Living in Space* would you like to read? What kind of information do you think is in the other chapters of the book?
2. What aspects of life aboard a spacecraft would be most difficult for you?
3. Do you have any interest in living in space? Why or why not? What is the longest amount of time you would want to spend in space? Why?

The planets

1   Earth is one of the nine planets that orbit around our life-giving star, the sun. Counting out from the sun, there are four *inner planets*. Rocky and smallish — on the cosmic scale, that is — they are also called the *terrestrial planets*.

2   **Mercury** Slightly larger than the Earth's moon, Mercury is too small to have its own atmosphere. Without an atmosphere to trap heat, Mercury is very cold, even though it is the planet nearest the sun.

3   **Venus** The planet closest in size to Earth, Venus is hidden by clouds. The temperature on Venus is hot enough at 850°F (500°C) to melt lead.

4   **Earth (and its moon)** The largest of the four terrestrial planets, Earth is the only one with liquid water on the surface.

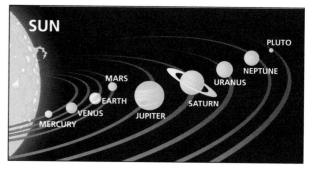

5   **Mars** Often called the Red Planet because the iron in its rocky surface has rusted, Mars has a distinctive reddish color. There are polar ice caps of dry ice (frozen carbon dioxide). Mars also has the solar system's largest mountain, an extinct volcano called Olympus Mons that is 17 miles high and 370 miles wide at its base.

6   The *outer planets* differ from the inner planets in that they may have a solid core but are surrounded by layers of liquid and gas.

7   **Jupiter** The largest planet spins rapidly — its "day" is only ten hours long. Like the sun, Jupiter is composed mainly of hydrogen and helium and has many moons — sixteen have been sighted so far.

8   **Saturn** With its famous rings, Saturn is probably the most recognizable planet. The second-largest planet, it has twenty-one moons. Those seven notable ring systems are made of mostly ice and rocks ranging in size from grains of dust to house-sized blocks.

9   **Uranus** The third-largest planet, it has fifteen moons and a series of dark rings. Unlike most other planets, Uranus spins "sideways."

10   **Neptune** Neptune is the fourth-largest planet. With eight known moons and its own set of rings, Neptune also features the highest surface winds in the solar system, measured at 1,500 miles per hour. Its large moon, Triton, has an atmosphere and is the coldest known place in the solar system, with temperatures as low as –390°F.

11   **Pluto** The ninth planet in our solar system is normally the planet farthest from the sun, usually about 3.7 billion miles. But an irregularity in its orbit brought Pluto temporarily into a position inside Neptune's orbit that lasted through the 1990s. This is one of the reasons Pluto is considered a planetary misfit. And unlike the other outer planets, it is small, cold, and rocky. Its one moon is called Charon. A current idea about Pluto is that it is either an asteroid, an escaped satellite of one of the other planets, or perhaps even a planet from another solar system that has been trapped inside our solar system.

Adapted from *Don't Know Much About Geography*.

Before you read

How much do you know about the planets in our solar system? Mark each statement true (*T*) or false (*F*).

_____ 1. Mercury is the planet nearest the sun.

_____ 2. Venus is the coldest planet.

_____ 3. Earth is the only planet that has liquid water on the surface.

_____ 4. Mars is red in color.

_____ 5. Jupiter has many moons.

_____ 6. Saturn is the largest planet.

_____ 7. Uranus is the smallest planet.

_____ 8. Neptune is the windiest planet.

_____ 9. Pluto is normally farthest from the sun.

Reading

Scan the text to check your answers. Then read the whole text.

After you read

A **Find the words in *italics* in the reading. Circle the meaning of each word.**

1. A *solid core* means the (hard center) / outer part of something. (par. 6)
2. When something *melts*, something solid becomes liquid / liquid becomes solid. (par. 3)
3. When something *spins*, it stays in the same place / turns around. (par. 7)
4. When something is *notable*, it is special and important / not unique. (par. 8)
5. *Grains of dust* are very large / small pieces. (par. 8)
6. A *misfit* is different from / the same as everything else. (par. 11)

B **Answer the questions.**

1. Which planets have a rocky surface?
2. Which planet may not be a true planet?
3. What are the four largest planets?
4. Which planets are cold?
5. Which planets have rings?
6. Which planets are surrounded by liquid and gas?
7. Which four planets are closest to the sun?

C **Answer these questions.**

1. Is it important for schoolchildren to learn about the solar system? Why or why not? How interested were you in learning about the solar system?
2. Do you think there is life on other planets? Is it important to find out? Why or why not?
3. Except for Earth, the names of the planets in English come from ancient Roman and Greek gods. Where do the names of the planets come from in your language?

Space tours not so far off

1 We're waiting to take trips to outer space. When will it happen? According to individuals in the growing field of space tourism, it may be in five or 50 years.

2 Space Adventures is taking reservations for the flights, similar to the first manned spaceflights. The trip will cost $90,000, with a $6,000 deposit required. More than 200 people have made reservations, said Sarah Dalton, the company spokeswoman.

3 John Spencer of the Space Tourism Society says that a more realistic estimate for regular space travel is 50 years. Issues of expense, difficulty, and danger must still be resolved. Oh yes — a reusable vehicle must also be invented.

4 He adds, however, that ten years from now, a limited number of people may be able to visit a space station. He said he expects a fleet of private space vehicles or "space yachts" to be in operation in 20 to 25 years. They will do what he calls "orbital super yachting." After that, there will be cruise lines, like those that travel the Earth's oceans, as well as space hotels and resorts.

5 There have been only a few studies to determine the public's interest in space tourism, but they all conclude that a majority of people would like to visit space and would be willing to pay good money for it.

6 According to expert Patrick Collins, between 5 million and 20 million people will head for space by 2030. He also predicts 100 flights a day leaving Earth.

7 It would be necessary to have more than 100 hotels in Earth's orbit, a few more orbiting the moon, and a few on the moon's surface. These hotels would employ more than 100,000 people, who would work month-long shifts.

8 Each hotel would have a service station. Such service stations would provide oxygen, water, and hydrogen. They might also ship environmentally safe electric power back to Earth. If all the issues can be resolved, Collins says that space tourism could one day become a $1 trillion industry.

READING TIP

Understanding prefixes and suffixes can help you understand the word's meaning. For example, the prefix *re-* means "again" and the suffix *-able* means "capable of." So, a *reusable vehicle* (par. 3) means "a vehicle that can be used again."

Adapted from *The Arizona Republic*.

Before you read

Check (✔) the questions you think the text will answer.

_____ 1. When will people start taking trips to outer space?

_____ 2. How much will a trip to outer space cost?

_____ 3. Why aren't people traveling to outer space now?

_____ 4. What will people wear in outer space?

_____ 5. Where will people stay in outer space?

_____ 6. How will people get oxygen and water?

Reading

Scan the text to check your predictions. Then read the whole text and answer the questions above.

After you read

A **Complete each sentence with a phrase from the boxes and the correct number. You may use phrases more than once.**

in _____ years   in _____ to _____ years

by _____   _____ years from now

1. Private space vehicles or "space yachts" might be in operation _in 20 to 25 years_.

2. There might be 100 flights a day leaving Earth _____.

3. People may be able to visit a space station _____.

4. According to John Spencer, people will make regular trips to space _____.

5. Millions of people might travel to space _____.

B **Find the words in _italics_ in the reading. Then match each word with its meaning.**

_d_ 1. _resolve_ (par. 3 and par. 8)   a. come to believe after studying some facts

_____ 2. _in operation_ (par. 4)   b. send something by air, train, boat, or truck

_____ 3. _conclude_ (par. 5)   c. go to

_____ 4. _willing_ (par. 5)   d. end a problem or difficulty

_____ 5. _head for_ (par. 6)   e. ready to do something

_____ 6. _ship_ (par. 8)   f. working

C **Answer these questions.**

1. Do you think space travel will become common for ordinary people in 100 years? Why or why not?

2. Would you like to work in outer space? What type of people would probably fill these jobs?

3. What do you think travelers to outer space will do for entertainment?

Vocabulary expansion

Skim the dictionary entries. Then find the correct definition for each word in *italics* in the sentences below.

1. **head** /hed/ *n* [C/U] the part of the body that contains the eyes, nose, mouth, ears, and the brain • *She nodded her head in agreement.*
2. **head** /hed/ *n* [C] the mind and mental abilities • *She has a good head for figures.*
3. **head** /hed/ *n* [C/U] a position or part at the top, front, or beginning • *They were early enough to get a place at the head of the line.*
4. **head** /hed/ *n* [C] someone who leads or is in charge of an organization or group, or this position of leadership • *In 1990 he was made head of the engineering division.*
5. **head** /hed/ *adj* [not gradable] main or most important • *In his first season as head coach, McGuire guided his team to the regional championship.*
6. **head** /hed/ *v* [I] to go in a particular direction • *I was heading out the door when the phone rang.*

7. **ship** /ʃɪp/ *n* [C] a boat, esp. one that is large enough to travel on the sea • *a cruise/cargo ship*
8. **ship** /ʃɪp/ *v* [T] - **pp** - to transport (something or someone) by air, train, boat, or truck • *They shipped our furniture from Tennessee.*

9. **operate** /ˈap·ə·reɪt/ *v* [I/T] to work or cause (something) to work, be in action, or have an effect • *How do you operate the remote control unit?*
10. **operation** /ap·əˈreɪ·ʃən/ *n* [C/U] • *Several printing presses are in operation (=working) at the moment.*
11. **operate** /ˈap·ə·reɪt/ *v* [I] to cut a body open in order to repair, remove, or replace an unhealthy or damaged part • *Doctors will operate on her tomorrow morning.*
12. **operation** /ap·əˈreɪ·ʃən/ *n* [C] *She underwent a six-hour open-heart operation.*

13. **space** /speɪs/ *n* [C/U] an empty place • *He was staring into space, seeing nothing.*
14. **space** /speɪs/ *v* [T] to arrange the distance between (things) • *Try to space the stitches evenly as you sew.*
15. **space** /speɪs/ *n* [U] the area beyond the ATMOSPHERE (=air) of the earth • *The rocket blasted off to outer space.*
16. **space** /speɪs/ *n* [U] an amount of time • *Within the space of three weeks, I felt much better.*

_6_ a. The newest spacecraft is going to *head* for Mars.

____ b. The *head* of the agency chooses the astronauts for each mission.

____ c. Astronauts usually have a good *head* for numbers.

____ d. They're going to *ship* parts of this old spacecraft to a museum.

____ e. The surgeon *operated* on the astronaut's arm when she returned to Earth.

____ f. I'm not interested in *space* travel.

____ g. In the *space* of a few minutes, the spacecraft was in orbit.

____ h. There isn't much *space* on a spacecraft.

Outer space and you

Work in groups. Imagine you are going to travel together for one week in outer space. Decide the following:

1. What are you going to do each day? How long is each activity going to last? What should you take with you?
2. Write a list of rules that must be followed by all members of the group while you are living in this small area.

9 Animals

You are going to read three texts about animals. First, answer the questions in the boxes.

READING 1

The terrible toads

This magazine article describes how toads, which were imported into Australia in 1935, have taken over parts of the Australian countryside.

1. Why do you think the toad was imported into Australia?
2. What problems do you think it causes? What other animals cause problems for people?

READING 2

Exotic animals — not as pets!

Many people like the idea of keeping wild animals as pets. Find out why it's not always such a good idea.

1. What kinds of animals do people in your country like to have as pets?
2. What kinds of animals do you think make the best pets? Which ones make the worst pets?

READING 3

Let's abandon zoos

Is it right or wrong to capture, cage, and display animals in zoos? This letter to the editor of a newspaper expresses one opinion.

1. When was the last time you went to the zoo?
2. Why do zoos exist? Do you think that they should continue to exist?

Vocabulary

Find out the meanings of the words in *italics*. Then answer the questions about these animals.

alligator	crocodile	insects	lizard	poodle	snake
bear	frog	koala	monkey	rabbit	turtle

1. Which animals can be *destructive*?
2. Which animals can be *poisonous*?
3. Which animals are *endangered* (in danger of becoming *extinct*)?
4. Which animals are *predators*?
5. Do the animals in the pictures belong to the same *species*?

THE TERRIBLE TOADS

Cane toads are guests who made themselves too much at home

1 When 100 marine toads were imported into Queensland, Australia, in 1935, farmers were optimistic. These marine toads were twice the length of a common toad, and farmers hoped that this large amphibian would control the beetles that were destroying their sugar cane crops. Before the toad came to Australia, its huge appetite for insects was useful in other parts of the world. Farmers in Puerto Rico, for example, brought the toads over from Central and South America to their sugar plantations. In this case, the toad was successful in keeping down the number of harmful pests.

Unlikely pets: Marine toads did little to control the beetles once destroying Australia's cane fields. But the 'cane toads' have made many friends, both young and old.

Disappointment

2 From the imported toads, authorities in Queensland raised 62,000 baby toads and released them into the cane fields. Unfortunately, they did not perform quite as expected. With Queensland's large supply of insects of all kinds, the toads paid no special attention to the destructive beetles. Moreover, with no natural predators in Australia, the toads soon spread throughout the region and the country.

3 In fact, predators that try to eat them are in for a nasty surprise. When the toads are held tightly, they squirt a poisonous spray from their shoulders. Some reports say they have killed crocodiles, koalas, lizards and snakes; people have also died after eating their poisonous flesh. In spite of this, many Queenslanders treat the toads as lovable pets. Others consider them awful creatures and kill them on sight.

Beetle

4 The "cane toads," as they became known, multiplied rapidly and are still going strong today. They don't seem to have damaged Australia's native ecology yet, and they continue to live happily alongside the local frogs.

> **READING TIP**
> Sometimes a word is replaced with a similar word to avoid repeating it. For example, *insects* and *pests* (par. 1) are two different nouns that have a similar meaning.

Adapted from *Did You Know?*

Before you read

Look at the large picture on the opposite page and the caption underneath it. Then check (✔) the information you think you will read about in the text.

_____ 1. The marine toads were imported into Australia in the 1930s to eat insects.

_____ 2. In Australia, the marine toads did not eat the insects they were supposed to eat.

_____ 3. The marine toad has many natural enemies in Australia.

_____ 4. The marine toads have caused serious damage to the native ecology.

_____ 5. The marine toads can be poisonous.

_____ 6. Not all Australians hate the cane toads.

Reading

Scan the text to check your predictions. Then read the whole text.

After you read

A **Number the sentences from 1 (first event) to 6 (last event).**

_____ a. Australians raised 62,000 baby toads.

_____ b. Farmers put toads into Australian sugar cane fields.

_1_ c. Farmers brought marine toads from Central and South America to Puerto Rico.

_____ d. Toads did not keep the number of beetles down.

_____ e. Marine toads kept the number of pests down in Puerto Rico.

_____ f. Farmers brought 100 marine toads to Australia.

B **Match each word or phrase with a word or phrase that is similar in meaning. (Note: Use one of the answers in column B twice.)**

A	B
_d_ 1. *pest* (par. 1)	a. *marine toad* (par. 1)
_____ 2. *this large amphibian* (par. 1)	b. *import* (par. 1)
_____ 3. *bring over* (par. 1)	c. *control* (par. 1)
_____ 4. *keep down* (par. 1)	d. *insect* (par. 1)
_____ 5. *cane toad* (par. 4)	e. *awful* (par. 3)
_____ 6. *nasty* (par. 3)	

C **Answer these questions.**

1. What does the story about the marine toads in Australia teach people?
2. Can you think of other animals that some people treat as "lovable pets" and other people think are "awful creatures"? What are they?
3. Are there any problems with animals in your country? Were these animals brought from other parts of the world, or are they native to your country? What are some possible solutions to the problems?

Exotic animals – not as pets!

1 Two years ago, George Watford, vice president at the Brooklyn, New York branch of the American Society for the Prevention of Cruelty to Animals (ASPCA), got a phone call about a female mountain lion living in a small apartment. The ASPCA went to check it out. "We didn't believe it," Watford said. "But when we went out there, sure enough, there's a mountain lion sitting at the front window looking out at us." Neighbors had complained about the mountain lion, and the big cat's owner didn't try to stop ASPCA officials who removed it and took it to an animal preserve.

2 If you think that cramped city apartments are a poor habitat for wild animals, you are right. That still doesn't stop some people from keeping just about any type of animal that they can fit inside their home. In one year, the ASPCA's city shelters took in 9,459 miscellaneous animals. The organization counts any animal that's not a cat or a dog as miscellaneous, so that number includes a lot of rabbits and turtles. However, the ASPCA has also recovered alligators, a leopard, and many other exotic pets.

3 It's illegal to sell wild animals or poisonous snakes in New York City. What's more, many apartment buildings don't even allow dogs and cats, let alone more exotic animals. Still, the ASPCA recovers most of its exotic animals not because someone complained, but because the pet's owner needed help. The cute lion or bear cub will eventually grow up to be a dangerous predator. "When they bite, it isn't because they hate you today. It's because they're wild animals," said Kathi Travers, ASPCA Director of Exotic Animals. She has the bite marks and scars to prove it.

4 Travers is quick to lecture against raising wild animals as pets. Too often, she says, people think that they can care for a wild animal as if it were a parrot or a poodle. "To love an animal is not enough," Travers said. "There has to be respect, and respect is not taking a squirrel monkey and sticking it in a little cage and expecting the animal to be happy."

Adapted from *Newsday*.

Predicting

Before you read

Check (✔) the reasons why you think exotic animals don't make good pets.

_____ 1. Wild animals can be dangerous.

_____ 2. Wild animals can make people ill.

_____ 3. Wild animals are not happy in small spaces.

_____ 4. It costs a lot of money to feed wild animals.

_____ 5. Wild animals behave badly in a home.

Scanning

Reading

Scan the text to check your predictions. Then read the whole text.

After you read

Understanding main ideas

A **Write the number of each paragraph next to its best heading.**

_____ a. There certainly are a lot of wild animals in people's homes.

_____ b. Don't try to keep a wild animal as a pet.

_____ c. Remember! Wild animals will always be wild.

__1__ d. Here is a very unusual story!

Making inferences

B **Complete the statements.**

1. When the ASPCA removed a mountain lion from an apartment in Brooklyn, New York, the animal's owners were _not unhappy_.
   a. very unhappy   b. not unhappy

2. Some people who keep wild baby animals as pets _____ about what the animals will be like when they grow up.
   a. think   b. do not think

3. It is _____ to keep a wild animal in New York.
   a. not legal   b. legal

4. Wild animals bite animal workers because the animals are _____.
   a. wild   b. angry

5. Animal workers think people should not keep _____ as a pet.
   a. any animal   b. any wild animal

Relating reading to personal experience

C **Answer these questions.**

1. Why do you think some people want an exotic animal, such as a mountain lion, a snake, or a monkey, as a pet?
2. What are some other possible problems with exotic animals that the article did not mention?
3. What should people do if they are no longer able to take care of a pet?

Let's abandon zoos

1 Where did we lose our compassion for living creatures? How could we possibly think that displaying animals in cages in unnatural environments — mostly for entertainment purposes — is fair and decent?

2 Zoo officials say they are concerned about animals. However, most zoos remain "collections" of interesting "items" rather than protective habitats. Zoos teach people that it is acceptable to keep animals in captivity — bored, cramped, lonely, and far from their natural homes.

3 Zoos claim to educate people and save endangered species, but visitors leave zoos without having learned anything meaningful about the animals' natural behavior, intelligence, or beauty. Most zoo enclosures are quite small, and most labels only mention the species' name, diet, and natural range. The animals' normal behavior is seldom observed, because zoos rarely take care of the animals' natural needs.

4 The animals are kept together in small spaces, with no privacy and little opportunity for mental stimulation or physical exercise. This results in abnormal and self-destructive behavior called zoochosis. A worldwide study of zoos conducted by the Born Free foundation revealed that zoochosis is common among animals kept in small spaces or cages. Another study found that elephants spend 22 percent of their time engaging in abnormal behaviors, such as repeated head movements or biting cage bars, and bears spend 30 percent of their time walking back and forth, a sign of distress.

5 Furthermore, most animals in zoos are not endangered. Captive breeding of endangered big cats, Asian elephants, and other species has not resulted in their release to the wild. Zoos talk a lot about their captive breeding programs because they do not want people to worry about a species becoming extinct. In fact, baby animals also attract a lot of paying customers. How many contests have we seen to name baby animals?

6 Ultimately, we will save endangered species only if we save their habitats and put an end to the reasons people kill them. Instead of supporting zoos, we should support groups that work to preserve animals' natural habitats.

Adapted from *The Buffalo News*.

Before you read

Do the adjectives have a positive or a negative meaning? Check (✔) the correct column.

	Positive	Negative		Positive	Negative
1. unnatural			5. bored		
2. fair			6. cramped		
3. decent			7. lonely		
4. protective			8. self-destructive		

Reading

Skim the text to check your predictions. Circle the statement that best describes the writer's opinion. Then read the whole text.

1. The writer thinks it is important for zoos to help save animals.
2. The writer thinks it is wrong to keep animals in zoos.

After you read

A **Find the words in *italics* in the reading. Circle the meaning of each word.**

1. *abandon* (title)
    a. continue using
    (b.) stop using

2. *compassion* (par. 1)
    a. feeling great love because something is beautiful
    b. feeling sadness for the problems of others

3. *captivity* (par. 2)
    a. a natural habitat
    b. an unnatural habitat

4. *mental stimulation* (par. 4)
    a. encouraging brain activity
    b. encouraging sleeping

5. *distress* (par. 4)
    a. interesting behavior
    b. great suffering

6. *breeding* (par. 5)
    a. adult animals having baby animals
    b. baby animals living in zoos

B **Read the complete sentences in the text again. Then write *fact* or *opinion*.**

1. Where did we lose . . . living creatures? (par. 1)   *opinion*
2. Zoos teach people . . . natural homes. (par. 2)   _____
3. Most zoo enclosures . . . natural range. (par. 3)   _____
4. A worldwide study . . . spaces or cages. (par. 4)   _____
5. Another study found . . . a sign of distress. (par. 4)   _____
6. Ultimately, we will save . . . people kill them. (par. 6)   _____

C **Answer these questions.**

1. Do you think zoos exist primarily to entertain people or to help save animals?
2. Do you think animals in zoos are "bored, cramped, and lonely"?
3. Do you agree with the writer of the letter? Why or why not?

Vocabulary expansion

A **Write the appropriate idiom under each picture.**

(be) a copycat
(be) in the doghouse

eat like a horse
fight like cats and dogs

Hold your horses!
It's raining cats and dogs.

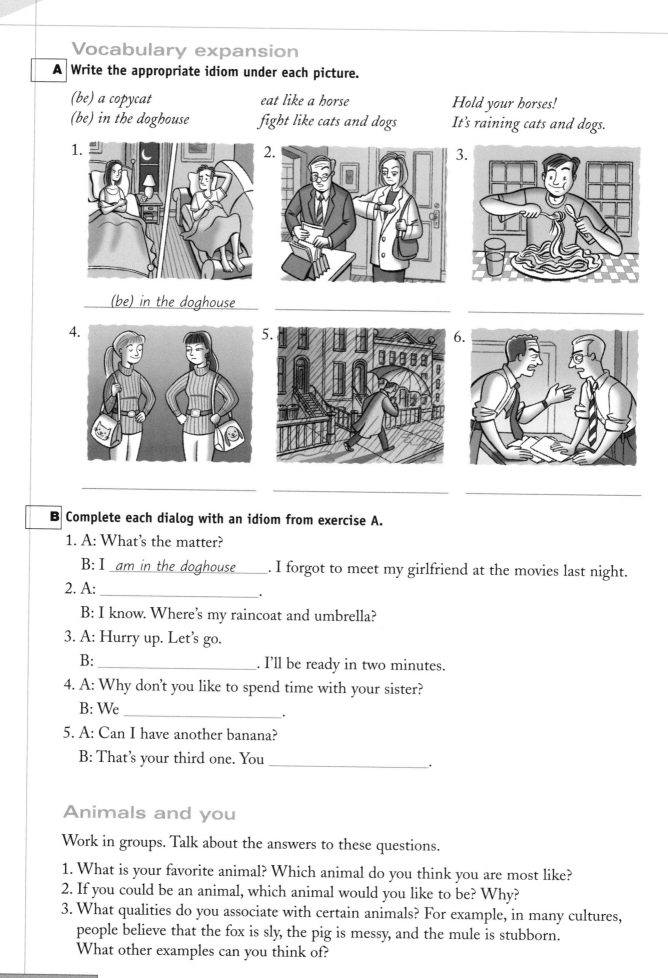

1.

_____(be) in the doghouse_____

2.

3.

4.

5.

6.

B **Complete each dialog with an idiom from exercise A.**

1. A: What's the matter?

   B: I _am in the doghouse_. I forgot to meet my girlfriend at the movies last night.

2. A: _____.

   B: I know. Where's my raincoat and umbrella?

3. A: Hurry up. Let's go.

   B: _____. I'll be ready in two minutes.

4. A: Why don't you like to spend time with your sister?

   B: We _____.

5. A: Can I have another banana?

   B: That's your third one. You _____.

Animals and you

Work in groups. Talk about the answers to these questions.

1. What is your favorite animal? Which animal do you think you are most like?
2. If you could be an animal, which animal would you like to be? Why?
3. What qualities do you associate with certain animals? For example, in many cultures, people believe that the fox is sly, the pig is messy, and the mule is stubborn. What other examples can you think of?

UNIT 10 Travel

You are going to read three texts about travel. First, answer the questions in the boxes.

READING 1

Adventure travel

Would you like to take a different kind of vacation? This guidebook suggests some interesting choices for travel destinations.

1. Do you like to travel? Why or why not?
2. If you could go anywhere in the world, where would you like to go? Why?

READING 2

Choosing an ecodestination

The development of tourism around the world can be harmful to the environment. This website describes places that preserve the environment.

1. Where did you go on your last vacation? What was the place like?
2. What are the most popular tourist spots in your country? Has tourism been good or bad for these places?

READING 3

Jet lag

Why do people feel bad for a few days after they travel long distances by airplane? Find out how long-distance travel affects the body.

1. Have you ever traveled a long distance in an airplane? If so, how did you feel the next day?
2. How do you think air travel affects people?

Vocabulary

Find out the meanings of the words in *italics*. Then check (✔) the vacation description that sounds the most interesting to you.

_____ 1. Travel to a *rain forest*. Explore the forest with *local guides*.

_____ 2. Stay at this beautiful *resort* on the Atlantic *coast*.

_____ 3. Enjoy the *bike paths*, beaches, and other *recreational* areas nearby.

_____ 4. Take part in some of the *traditional ceremonies* of the region.

_____ 5. Take a tour of this *scenic* countryside and see some of the world's greatest *architectural* and *natural wonders*.

Adventure travel

1 Morocco
Trek to the heart of the high Atlas

The Atlas is the highest mountain range in North Africa. The villages of the Berbers — a very independent people — are situated on the steep hillsides. After two days in the city of Marrakech, members of the tour group start their trek from the green Mizzane Valley. They follow ancient mule trails into the mountains. They spend the nights in the traditional stone, wood, and mud houses of Berber villages. Travelers share the food and accommodation of their friendly hosts. They sip green mint tea with the local people and watch their traditional dances. The highlight of the trip is a climb to the top of Mount Toubkal. At 13,670 feet, it is the highest point in North Africa. Mules carry all baggage.

2 Vietnam
A mountain-bike tour of the Vietnamese countryside

Bicycles are probably the best way for foreign visitors to meet the people of Vietnam. After all, bicycles are the way most rural Vietnamese get around. Travelers on this tour visit many of the beautiful, cultural, and historic sights of the country. Bicyclists can ride along the wide boulevards of Ho Chi Minh City and visit the amazing tunnel complex of CuChi. They also travel along the South China Sea coast past pagodas, or temples, beaches, old French villas, and charming fishing villages. The bike tour includes a visit to Hoi An, a well-preserved sixteenth-century town. The tour finishes in Hanoi, which is much more traditional than Ho Chi Minh City.

3 Ecuador
Diving the Galapagos Islands

Divers swim with sea lions, seals, sea turtles, penguins, and other magnificent creatures. There is nowhere else like it. These remote islands are the most unusual dive destinations in the world. Divers live aboard a luxurious boat, which offers plenty of stops to enjoy the wonders of the islands. There are also professional naturalist guides on board and plenty of opportunities to visit the shore.

4 France
By hot-air balloon over the Loire Valley

Here in the center of France is one of the greatest collections of architectural wonders in the whole world. There are over 1,000 magnificent châteaux, or castles, and manor houses among vineyards, orchards, and forests. Travelers float at treetop level in cheerfully colored hot-air balloons over one of the most scenic regions in France. They enjoy a marvelous opportunity to see details of architectural beauty and formal gardens that they cannot observe from the ground. The trip includes tours of several of the most famous châteaux.

Adapted from *The Big Book of Adventure Travel.*

Before you read

Look at the pictures from Morocco, Vietnam, Ecuador, and France. Then write the name of the country under each picture.

1. _____
2. _____
3. _____
4. _____

Reading

Skim the text to check your predictions. Then read the whole text.

After you read

A **Correct the mistake in each statement.**

the mountains

1. The travelers in Morocco spend most of their time in Marrakech.

2. During the trip to Morocco, mules carry the travelers.

3. Travelers to Vietnam travel by boat around the country during some of the trip.

4. Divers around the Galapagos Islands can see lions and sea turtles.

5. Travelers to the Loire Valley take a tour of several of the most famous vineyards and orchards.

B **Check (✔) the correct column.**

	Morocco	Vietnam	Ecuador	France
1. Which trip(s) do *not* require physical fitness?				✔
2. Which trip(s) require special training?				
3. During which trip(s) will travelers see cities?				
4. During which trip(s) will travelers spend time with local people?				
5. Which trip(s) are good for travelers who like to see beautiful, old homes and/or monuments?				

C **Answer these questions.**

1. Do you think adventure travel sounds interesting? Why or why not?
2. Which of the trips in the reading would you rather take? Why? Why didn't you choose the other trips?
3. What places in your country are good for adventure travel?

Choosing an ecodestination

1 Imagine visiting an uncrowded, beautifully preserved coastline or rain forest. A local guide is ready and able to explain the natural wonders before you. Imagine relaxing among local people who are genuinely happy to meet you and share their world. This vision is no fantasy. Vacations for environmentally and culturally aware travelers are available in many locations around the world.

Real-life examples!

2 In Brazil, an ecoresort on the coast of Bahia helps to save the Atlantic rain forest, one of the most endangered on earth. Visitors can explore the forest with "mini guides," local children who take great pride in the beauty of their forest. Visitors can also spend time at a sea turtle breeding facility next to the resort. Here they can learn how villagers protect the nesting sea turtles every night on the beach in front of the tourists' hotel.

3 Off the coast of Western Samoa — a Pacific island known for its unique culture and exotic scenery — lies a very special small island. On this island, local villagers still fish in the early morning hours and weave their nets during the day. Villagers warmly welcome visitors by preparing meals of fresh, local seafood. Later, guests are invited to take part in a ceremonial dance on the beach under the stars. After the ceremony, guests retire to a locally owned lodge and enjoy the sounds of the South Sea.

What to look for in an ecodestination

4 • Destinations that are not overcrowded or overdeveloped

• Plenty of protected landscapes and recreational areas, such as bike paths or beach areas, that are shared by locals and visitors alike

• Successful, locally owned hotels, restaurants, and businesses that provide genuine hospitality and friendly staff

• Local control over tourism development that is not harmful to the environment

• Local festivals and events that demonstrate the locals' pride in their environment and culture

Adapted from *www.ecotourism.org.*

Before you read

An *ecodestination* is a place where travelers go, but where their visit will not damage the
environment. Check (✔) the statements you think are true.

_____ 1. Travelers visit destinations that are not crowded.

_____ 2. Travelers see and learn about natural wonders of the area.

_____ 3. Travelers stay in luxury hotels.

_____ 4. Travelers help support local businesses.

_____ 5. Travelers do some environmental work with local people.

_____ 6. Travelers tour in large, guided groups.

Reading

Scan the text to find out which statements above describe an ecodestination. Then read
the whole text.

After you read

A Check (✔) the statements that describe *both* ecodestinations in the text.

✓ 1. They are on the coast.

_____ 2. They have guides that show visitors the region.

_____ 3. They teach visitors about local wildlife.

_____ 4. They allow visitors to spend time with the local people.

_____ 5. They offer planned activities for the visitors.

B Check (✔) the statements that describe people who would probably enjoy an
ecodestination.

_____ 1. Sofia enjoys getting to know the great cities of the world.

✓ 2. Tom and Louise are interested in taking their children on a trip where the
family will learn something about animal and/or plant life.

_____ 3. David prefers places where he can spend time with the people who live there.

_____ 4. Jessica and her boyfriend want to go to a place with an exciting nightlife.

_____ 5. Carol and Bob want to go to a beach resort abroad, but they prefer staying in
American-owned hotels.

_____ 6. Chris gets upset when she sees how tourists have damaged the environment.

C Answer these questions.

1. Would you rather visit the ecoresort in Brazil or the small island off the coast of
Western Samoa? Which sounds more interesting? Why?

2. Where should travelers in your country go if they want to visit an ecodestination?

3. Would you prefer going to an ecodestination or to a place most tourists like to visit?

Jet lag

1   What has ruined more vacations? What has been the reason for more unsuccessful business meetings after a long trip? What has caused more problems for the air traveler than all the other irritations of flying? Jet lag.

2   What is jet lag? It comes from traveling a long distance in an east/west direction to a new time zone. The travel time is too fast for the human body to easily adjust. Air travel disrupts three important senses: the sense of place, the sense of time, and, as a result of both, the sense of well-being.

3   **Sense of place** To some extent, all locations are physically, geographically, and even chemically different from one another. All humans, like all living things, have a strong sense of place, either consciously or unconsciously. Consciously, this makes people homesick for familiar surroundings and wish for their own bed. Unconsciously, people miss the usual hometown patterns of something as simple as the familiar timing of sunrise and sunset.

4   **Sense of time** All people have a natural sense of time that is connected to their sense of place. Our bodies function on a program that takes about a day to run, and they sense the different qualities of 6:00 A.M., noon, and midnight.

5   **Sense of well-being** The sense of well-being is completely dependent on sense of time and sense of place. A change in the sense of time, sense of place, or both, causes a disruption in a person's sense of well-being.

6   For 250,000 years, the human's sense of well-being, as connected to sense of time and sense of place, did not change. People could go no faster than their own feet could take them, their animals could carry them, or their boats could transport them. They took weeks, months, years, or generations to travel great distances around the earth.

7   It was the coming of the airplane that changed all this and created something completely new — jet lag. Because people could travel by air, there were no more of the geographic restrictions that existed before humans could leave the earth. However, humans still possess an essentially Stone Age body that should be traveling great distances very, very slowly, if at all. Therefore, they suffer the consequences in the form of jet lag.

> **READING TIP**
> Sometimes the parts of a word can help you understand it. For example, *well* in *well-being* is connected to *healthy* and *good*; *being* is the present participle of *be*. So, *well-being* describes a person's health and happiness.

Adapted from *Overcoming Jet Lag*.

Before you read

Look at the headings on the opposite page. Then check (✔) what you think the text will be about.

_____ 1. how people feel when they have jet lag

_____ 2. why people get jet lag

_____ 3. what people can do to avoid getting jet lag

Reading

Skim the text to check your prediction. Then read the whole text.

After you read

A **Find the words in *italics* in the reading. Circle the meaning of each word.**

1. *adjust* (par. 2)
   a. travel very quickly to a place that is far away
   (b.) change a little to make something work well

2. *disrupt* (par. 2)
   a. stop something from continuing as usual
   b. continue something as usual

3. *sense* (par. 2–6)
   a. the meaning of something
   b. a feeling

4. *consciously* (par. 3)
   a. with thoughts that you are not aware of
   b. with thoughts that you are aware of

5. *run* (par. 4)
   a. move the legs faster than when walking
   b. start and continue until the end

6. *Stone Age* (par. 7)
   a. 100 years ago
   b. 250,000 years ago

7. *geographic* (par. 7)
   a. related to the location of places on the earth
   b. related to the problems that come from traveling

B **Complete the summaries. Then circle the paragraph that best summarizes the text.**

1. People suffer from jet lag when they _travel a long distance in an east/west direction to a new time zone_. They get jet lag because there has been a change in their _____, _____, and _____.

2. People have a sense of well-being if there is no change in their _____ and/or _____. People's sense of well-being did not change before they could travel by plane because _____ _____.

C **Answer these questions.**

1. Have you ever had jet lag? If so, how did it affect you?
2. Do you think jet lag is a serious problem? Do you know some ways to avoid it?
3. What are some "irritations" of traveling you have experienced?

Vocabulary expansion

A Write the appropriate words under each postcard below. (Some words can be used more than once.) Then add one more word under each postcard.

a bathing suit	go fishing	a guidebook	suntan lotion
a campground	go hiking/hike	a ski lodge	take lots of pictures
a chair lift	go skiing/ski	skis	a tent
get a suntan	go sightseeing	sunbathe	a tour guide
get sunburned	go swimming/swim		

1.

a bathing suit

2.

3.

4.

B Where would you like to be right now? Write a postcard from that place.

Travel and you

Work in groups. Make a magazine or newspaper advertisement for a vacation spot in your country. What picture or pictures are you going to use? What are you going to say in the ad? (You can use the advertisements on page 74 as examples.)

11 The Internet

You are going to read three texts about the Internet. First, answer the questions in the boxes.

READING 1

Love on the Internet

Read this newspaper article to find out how young people use the Internet as a matchmaking service.

1. Why do you think people use the Internet to make friends or look for romance?
2. What can you find out about someone on the Internet? What can you hide from someone?

READING 2

Help on the Internet

This magazine article tells the remarkable true story of a Finnish girl whose life was saved by sending a message for help on the Internet.

1. Do you ever visit Internet chat rooms? If so, which ones?
2. Would you believe the stories of someone you met in an Internet chat room? Why or why not?

READING 3

Count me out

In this newspaper editorial, the writer explains why he does not think much of what the Internet can do for him.

1. What do you use the Internet for? If you do not use the Internet, would you like to use it? Why or why not?
2. What do you think people will be able to do on the Internet in the future?

Vocabulary

Find out the meanings of the words in *italics*. Then check (✔) the statements that are true about you.

_____ 1. I *log on* to the Internet every day.

_____ 2. I use *e-mail* to communicate with people in different parts of the world.

_____ 3. I buy a lot of things on *the Web*.

_____ 4. There are several *websites* I really like.

_____ 5. I like to go into *chat rooms* so I can practice using English.

Love on the Internet

1   Caught between his traditional family and his Californian lifestyle, Tariq Ahmed found the perfect way to arrange his own marriage — by finding a wife on the Web. Along with thousands of other young Asians, the 27-year-old Silicon Valley computer expert turned to the growing number of Internet sites dedicated to finding a suitable husband or wife.

2   Born in London to a Pakistani father and an Austrian mother, Mr. Ahmed, a designer of Web pages, had little difficulty producing his own site. He admits that, like all his Pakistani friends in the U.S.A., he had to do something about his love life. "My dad has become extremely conservative over the years, and he just wanted me to marry a Pakistani girl," he said.

3   She turned out to be 26-year-old Juliana Gidwani. She saw his advertisement on the Matrimonial Link. They married last year near her home. The wedding pictures, of course, were immediately posted on the Web.

4   "The Internet isn't ideal because you have to use e-mails and when you are talking in text you are only getting a bit of information." Ahmed added that e-mails can't show two people whether there is chemistry between them. Luckily, he and his bride discovered they did have chemistry after they spent some time getting to know each other.

5   Speed and control are what is important in e-mail relationships. Websites and e-mail addresses allow people to choose the level of anonymity they wish to keep. They also can select people who live far away.

6   Sara, 27, was born in India and is studying in the U.S.A. After her parents' matchmaking attempts failed, she began her own search. She registered with the Internet agency A1 Indian Matrimonials. She had many replies and quickly found a potential husband. "He's a doctor, a real golden boy with a flood of proposals from good families, which his parents have gone nuts trying to get him to accept."

Adapted from *The Times*.

Before you read

Check (✔) the statements you agree with.

A good thing about looking for a spouse on the Internet is that . . .

_____ 1. you can get to know a person completely.

_____ 2. you can find out easily if you and the other person have chemistry.

_____ 3. you can get responses quickly.

_____ 4. you are in control.

_____ 5. if you want, your identity can be completely anonymous, or private.

_____ 6. there is more choice.

Reading

**Scan the text to find the advantages of looking for a spouse on the Internet. Then read
the whole text.**

After you read

A | Complete the summary.

Tariq Ahmed was born in _____London_____. He was living in _____ when he

decided to look for a wife on the Internet. He was _____ old at the time. His

website was with an Internet agency called _____. Through the Internet, he met

and married _____. She was _____ old at the time.

Sara was born in _____ and is living in _____. _____

tried to find a spouse for her but didn't succeed. She is using an Internet agency called

_____.

B | Check (✔) the statements that are true.

__✓__ 1. It was important for Tariq to marry someone of the same background.

_____ 2. Tariq and his wife are happily married.

_____ 3. Tariq's father was happy about Tariq's marriage.

_____ 4. It is important for Sara to marry someone from the same country.

_____ 5. Sara got married.

C | Answer these questions.

1. What are some disadvantages of marrying someone you meet on the Internet?
   What are the advantages of using the Internet to meet a spouse?
2. Imagine you are going to list information about yourself on the Internet.
   What will you say about yourself?
3. How important is it for you to marry someone from the same country? Why?

Help on the Internet

1 One day, 12-year-old Sean Redden logged on to the Internet. He went to a popular chat room called Glenshadows Tavern. There weren't any people in the chat room. Just as he was about to sign off and do something else, he saw the name of someone he'd never seen there before, Susan Hicks. Her brief message was "Would someone help me?"

2 Sean typed back, "What's wrong?" A moment later he received this message, "I can't breathe. Help me! I can't feel my left side. I can't get out of my chair."

3 *Oh, man,* Sean thought. Pretending to be paralyzed was a bad joke. Then he wondered, *What if she really is sick? I've got to help.* "Hey, Mom," he called. "There's a kid here who's sick or something."

4 Sharon Redden looked at the computer screen. "It's not just some game, is it?" she asked.

5 The message was not a joke. "Susan Hicks" was actually 20-year-old Taija Laitinen, a student working late at night at a college library near Helsinki, Finland — almost 7,000 miles away from Sean's home in Texas. While searching the Internet, she began to feel terrible pain all through her body. What could she do? The library was silent and empty. The nearest phone was outside in the hallway. She couldn't move that far. Any movement caused the pain to get worse.

6 Then she realized that she might get help on the Internet. But how? Taija sometimes practiced her English in Glenshadows Tavern. As the pain got worse, she logged on using her Web name and began typing her message for help.

7 "I don't think it's a joke, Mom," Sean said. He looked at Susan's last message, and he typed, "Where are you?" After a long pause, the letters appeared: "Finland." Sean and Sharon couldn't believe it. Not knowing what else to do, Sharon called the local police.

8 Sharon explained the situation to officer Amy Schmidt. Schmidt told Sharon to try to get the sick girl's phone number.

9 Sean asked several times for the girl's phone number and location. Finally, a message with her number and address came back. Texas police called the international telephone operator and asked to be connected to the proper agency in Finland. The call was transferred to a nearby rescue station. The Texas police explained the situation and gave Susan's address to the Finnish operator. When Sean heard that, he typed, "Help is on the way."

10 In a few minutes, Taija heard people running down the hallway outside the door. Suddenly, the door opened. Emergency workers and three policemen ran in. Taija turned once more to the computer, "They are here. Thanks. Bye-bye."

11 Four days later, the police in Texas received a message from officers in Finland: "Thanks to her Internet friend, Taija had received medical treatment she badly needed and is doing well."

Adapted from *Reader's Digest.*

Before you read

Predicting

Look at these words and phrases from the text. What do you think happens in the story?

chat room	Mom	Web name	international operator
"What's wrong?"	college library	Finland	emergency workers
paralyzed	feel terrible pain	local police	medical treatment

Reading

Scanning

Scan the text to check your prediction. Then read the whole text.

After you read

Understanding a sequence of events

A **Number the sentences from 1 (first event) to 10 (last event).**

_____ a. Texas police called the international operator.

_____ b. Sean's mother called the police in Texas.

_1_ c. Sean logged on to his computer.

_____ d. Sean began receiving messages from someone named "Susan."

_____ e. "Susan" heard footsteps outside her door.

_____ f. Sean found out where "Susan" was.

_____ g. The international operator connected Texas police to the police in Finland.

_____ h. Sean showed his mother that someone on the Internet was asking for help.

_____ i. Sean entered a chat room.

_____ j. Sean received a message that said that help had arrived.

Understanding details

B **Correct the mistake in each statement.**

          didn't believe

1. At first, Sean believed the person sending the message for help was really sick.

2. Susan Hicks was a friend of Taija Laitinen.

3. Susan was in a chat room that day to practice her English.

4. Susan didn't phone for help because there was no telephone in the building.

5. Sean didn't know help was coming before Susan told him help had arrived.

6. Susan got medical treatment for an illness that was not serious.

Relating reading to personal experience

C **Answer these questions.**

1. What do you think the Texas police thought when they received the call from Sean's mother? Why do you think they decided to take the phone call seriously?
2. Do you think Sean and Taija still communicate with each other? Why or why not?
3. Do you use the Internet to practice English? If so, how? If not, would you like to?

Count me out

1 Call me old-fashioned. Call me old. Call me what you want, but I refuse to become part of this new Internet world.

2 I do not possess a computer at home or at the office. Actually, I stopped going to an office 35 years ago, when all communications were done in a relaxed manner, with a pen, a typewriter, or, if the matter was of world-shaking importance, over the telephone. Likewise, if you liked something advertised in a newspaper or magazine, you visited the shop selling it at the given address, or you phoned the number shown. Then you spoke to a fellow human and asked for further details.

3 Tell me what you think of the following ad that appeared the other day in the newspaper. It was for a cure for cancer and this is what it said: "Awareness is the key. Visit spfulford.com at the awareness site." There was no address or telephone number for the site. So what do unfortunate people without a computer do if they are seeking a cure for their illness?

4 There are, I am told, certain advantages in having access to the latest marvel of the age, the Internet. I have no idea how it works, but you can, for example, send love messages across the world or even get married to someone that you meet online. This bit doesn't interest me; I have been happily married for 60 years. There are, of course, other activities for Internet users besides finding love. They can pay bills, order groceries, or discuss illnesses with their doctor.

5 And this is by no means all. More amazing things are yet to come in the near future. I read a newspaper report recently that quoted Stephen Hawking, an important British scientist. "The complexity of a computer as it exists today is probably less than the brain of an earthworm," he said. "But, as technology advances, computers will become more complex, and a time may come when the Internet may develop 'consciousness.' In other words, the Internet will be able to think, have feelings, and may well be able to act on its own."

6 If Professor Hawking is right, I may change my attitude about computers. As I grow older each day, I would like a gadget that not only thinks for me but also accepts responsibility for all my mistakes.

> **READING TIP**
> Quotation marks (" ") show that a word has a special meaning in a specific context that is a little different from the meaning in the dictionary. For example, the meaning of *consciousness* is "ability to think, have feelings, and to act on one's own."

Adapted from *The Statesman*.

Before you read

Count me out means "don't include me." Check (✔) the statement that you think best expresses the writer's opinion.

_____ 1. There are many things people can do on the Internet.

_____ 2. People will be able to do more things on the Internet in the future.

_____ 3. The writer can live without the Internet.

_____ 4. There is nothing good about the Internet.

Reading

Skim the text to check your prediction. Then read the whole text.

After you read

A What is the writer's attitude toward the Internet? Check (✔) the correct answer.

_____ 1. angry   _____ 3. sarcastic

_____ 2. sad   _____ 4. serious

B Find the words in *italics* in the reading. Then complete the sentences.

old-fashioned (par. 1)   *cure* (par. 3)   *complex* (par. 5)   *attitude* (par. 6)   *gadget* (par. 6)

1. A car is not a simple machine. Many people don't realize cars are so _complex_.
2. This _____ will help you remember to do things. It's a useful machine.
3. People say I have the wrong _____, but I think my opinion is right.
4. My children say I'm _____. They think that my ideas are from the past.
5. Too bad there isn't a _____ for the illness. Doctors can't help everybody.

C Answer the questions.

1. How did people communicate with each other when the writer was younger?
   People communicated with each other by writing letters or talking on the telephone.
2. What did the writer think was wrong with the Internet ad for a cancer cure?

   _____

3. What are three things that people do on the Internet?

   _____

4. How might the Internet be different in the future?

   _____

5. What would the writer like a computer to do for him?

   _____

D Answer these questions.

1. Which of the writer's points do you agree and/or disagree with?
2. What do you think computers will never be able to do for people?
3. In what ways do computers and the Internet have a negative effect on society? In what ways do they have a positive effect?

Vocabulary expansion

A Find the phrasal verbs below in this unit's readings. Then write the letter of the correct definition next to each phrasal verb.

_c_ 1. *turn to* (reading 1, par. 1)

_____ 2. *turn out* (reading 1, par. 3)

_____ 3. *log on* (reading 2, par. 1)

_____ 4. *sign off* (reading 2, par. 1)

_____ 5. *get out of* (reading 2, par. 2)

_____ 6. *count me out* (reading 3, title)

a. change the direction of your body
b. end a letter or message
c. get help from
d. end in a particular way
e. don't include me

f. move out of a space
g. receive
h. say *1, 2, 3*
i. write your name in a particular way
j. enter a computer system by using a password

B Complete each sentence with a phrasal verb from exercise A.

1. When you don't know what to do, you should _____ *turn to* _____ the teacher.

2. I'm going to _____ now. I don't have anything else to say.

3. Don't worry about the test. Everything will _____ OK.

4. Before I can check my e-mail messages, I have to _____.

5. I was very tired this morning and just couldn't _____ bed.

6. _____. I don't want to play any computer games.

The Internet and you

If you have Internet access:
Make a presentation about your favorite website. Show some printouts from the site. Describe the different parts of the website, and explain why you like them.

If you do not have Internet access:
Working with another student, talk about things you would like to know about the Internet. Make a list of questions. Then, if you know someone who has Internet access, ask your questions. Report the person's answers to the class.

UNIT

12 Friends

You are going to read three texts about friendship. First, answer the questions in the boxes.

READING 1

Ten easy ways to make friends

This magazine offers some practical advice for anyone who would like to make more friends.

1. Do you find it easy or difficult to make new friends? Why?
2. What qualities does a good friend have?

READING 2

Best friends

What does it mean to have a best friend? This introduction from a book called *Best Friends* has the answers.

1. How is a best friend different from all other friends?
2. Are male friendships different from female friendships? If so, how?

READING 3

The new family

Are friends more important to us than our own family? This newspaper article explains why for many people, the answer is "yes."

1. How many close friends do you have? How many are male? How many are female?
2. Who do you spend more time with, family or friends? How are friendships different from the relationships we have with family members?

Vocabulary

Find out the meanings of the words in *italics*. Then check (✔) the statements you agree with.

In a good friendship,...	Very important	Somewhat important	Not very important
there is *intimacy*.			
there is *trust*.			
there is *commitment*.			
there is *loyalty*.			
friends are *supportive*.			
friends are *caring*.			

Ten easy ways to make *friends*

1 It's hard to make friends if you stay home alone all the time. Get out of the house and do things that will put you in touch with other people. Join a club or play a sport. Attend meetings of neighborhood associations or other groups. It's easier to make friends when you have similar interests.

2 Learn from people at school or work who seem to have lots of friends. Observe how they make and keep friends. Don't imitate all of the things they do, but try to notice what they do. Then try some of those things yourself.

3 Don't be afraid to show people what you're really good at. Talk about the things you like and do best. Don't hide your strong points. People will be interested in you if there is something interesting about you.

4 Plan things to talk about with people. Find out what's in the newspaper headlines, listen to the top CDs, learn about what's new with your favorite TV or movie star. The more you have to say, the more people will be interested in having a conversation with you.

5 Look people in the eye when you talk to them. That way, they'll find it easier to talk to you. It's very difficult to have a conversation with people whose eyes are looking to the left, to the right, at the floor — anywhere but in the other person's face. People may think you're not interested in them and may stop being interested in you.

6 Be a good listener. Let people talk about themselves before talking about "me, me, me." Ask lots of questions. Show an interest in their answers. This alone will make people want to be your friend.

7 Once you start to get to know someone, don't be friendly one day and then too shy to talk the next day. Be consistent. Consistency is something people look for in friends.

8 Have confidence in yourself. Don't be self-critical all the time. This will only make the process more difficult. Think of your good qualities. People are attracted to those with self-confidence.

9 Try to make friends with the kind of people you really like, respect, and admire — not just with those who are easy to meet. Be friendly with a lot of people. That way, you'll have a bigger group of people to choose from and have greater chances for making friends.

10 After you make a new friend, keep him or her by being a good friend. Treat your friend as you would like him or her to treat you. Be loyal, caring, and supportive. Your friend will treat you the same way.

Adapted from *'Teen*.

Predicting
Before you read
Write down three pieces of advice you think you will read in the text.

1. _____
2. _____
3. _____

Scanning
Reading
Scan the text to check your predictions. Then read the whole text.

Making inferences
After you read

A **What advice in the article do these people need to follow? Write the correct number for each person.**

___4___ a. Tony is never sure what to talk about when he meets people.

_____ b. Rose wants to know why her classmate, Cindy, is so good at making friends.

_____ c. When Pedro feels uncomfortable talking to someone, he starts to look away.

_____ d. Abby doesn't always say nice things about her new friend, James.

_____ e. Terry wants to be friends with the most popular girl in class because everyone else likes her.

_____ f. Adam stays home every Saturday night and watches videos.

_____ g. Jill often asks herself, "Why would anyone want to be my friend?"

_____ h. Benson is a terrific dancer, but he never tells anyone about it.

_____ i. Martha always talks about herself.

_____ j. Max talks to a girl in his algebra class on Monday, but on Tuesday he's afraid to say "Hi."

Guessing meaning from context
B **Find the words in *italics* in the reading. Circle the meaning of each word.**

1. When you are *put in touch with* other people, you **meet** / **touch** other people. (par. 1)
2. When you *observe* something, you **write it down** / **watch it**. (par. 2)
3. When you *imitate* something, you **look at** / **copy** it. (par. 2)
4. Your *strong points* are **good** / **bad** things about you. (par. 3)
5. When you are *consistent*, you do things in **different ways** / **the same way**. (par. 7)
6. When you *admire* someone, you **have a good opinion of** / **love** the person. (par. 9)
7. When you *treat* someone well, you are **happy to be with** / **nice to** the person. (par. 10)

Relating reading to personal experience
C **Answer these questions.**

1. What advice in the article do you think is the most helpful?
2. Do you disagree with any of the advice in the article?
3. What other advice would you give to someone who wanted to make more friends?

Best friends

1   Men and women share the exact same view of a best friend — a person who is always there for you. Your best friend is someone you can depend on to share your happiness, suffer through your worries, or lessen your sorrow. As one man put it, "To me, a best friend is somebody that you call if you're on the expressway and get a flat tire at 3:00 A.M. and you've been told it's four hours until a tow truck can be sent. Your friend says, 'Tell me exactly where you are, and I'll come and get you.'"

2   A great variety of factors play into the birth of a best friendship — the age and circumstances under which people meet, what first attracts them, why they remain close, and how they fill each other's needs. Yet I found the dominant themes that define a best friend were remarkably similar across the broadest range of experiences.

3   *Safety* was a word I heard over and over. A best friend is a safe harbor, a guaranteed comfort zone. You never have to explain yourself to best friends because they really, really know who you are. With best friends, you can be who you are. You can cry too hard or laugh too loud and never worry what they'll think of you because best friends are *nonjudgmental*. They will give you advice if you want it and a kick in the pants if you need it, but best friends will not judge you or make you ashamed of your behavior. A best friend gives you what you expect from a parent and don't always get: *unconditional love*.

4   Best friends are *loyal* and *trustworthy*. A best friend is a person to whom you can tell your most embarrassing, revealing, and damaging personal secrets with the full confidence they will never be repeated. Best friends can deliver brutally *honest* answers in the most gentle fashion.

5   Finally, best friends are the *family you choose*. They love you because they want to, not because they have to. And for many people, a best friend becomes the brother or sister they'd always wanted, but never had.

6   A man I knew asked his dying mother, "What has been the most important thing in your life?" He fully expected her to say her husband, her children, or her family. Instead, without a moment's hesitation, she replied sweetly, "My friends."

Adapted from *Best Friends*.

Before you read

Look at these expressions from the text. Then check (✔) what you think the text will be about.

someone you can depend on

a safe harbor

never have to explain yourself

a kick in the pants

will not judge you

unconditional love

_____ 1. The writer talks about how she met her best friend.

_____ 2. Different people talk about the difference between a friend and a best friend.

_____ 3. The writer talks about the qualities of a best friend.

Reading

Skim the text to check your prediction. Then read the whole text.

After you read

A **Check (✔) the statements that are true.**

_✓_ 1. Best friends always help when there is a problem.

_____ 2. Best friends have similar interests.

_____ 3. Best friends really know each other.

_____ 4. People know their best friend will not tell anybody their secrets.

_____ 5. Best friends don't have arguments.

_____ 6. Best friends are like family.

B **Read the complete sentences in the text again. Then check (✔) the correct column.**

	Main idea	Supporting information
1. Men and women . . . there for you. (par. 1)	✓	
2. "To me, a best friend . . . come and get you." (par. 1)		
3. You can cry . . . are nonjudgmental. (par. 3)		
4. With best friends, . . . who you are. (par. 3)		
5. Best friends . . . trustworthy. (par. 4)		
6. A best friend . . . never be repeated. (par. 4)		

C **Answer these questions.**

1. How long have you known your best friend (or a good friend)?

2. How did you meet this friend? What do you remember about the first time you met? Why do you think you are so close?

3. Which of the qualities mentioned in this article are true about your relationship with your best friend?

The new family

0

1 When the telephone rings late at night, most women guess it must be one of only four or five people calling. A sister? Maybe. An emergency? Possibly. A mother? Probably not at that time of night. Much more likely it is a close female friend — someone calling to tell you that she has split up with her boyfriend again or perhaps simply that a good movie has just started on TV.

2 At a time when families are spread far and wide and marriages often end in divorce, friendships of intimacy and trust are becoming more and more important. Erika, a 32-year-old lawyer, is strengthened by her ten-year friendship with her married friend Jane. "I was very sick one night, and so I called Jane at about 3:00 A.M. to talk about it," she says. "She was very supportive and even came over to take me to the doctor's the next morning."

3 As American TV shows like *Friends*, which follows the lives of a very close group of young friends, have become more popular, many of us are beginning to see the value of such friendships. TV shows like this tell us that our romantic relationships may not last, but we need to keep in touch with our close friends if we want to survive.

4 A TV show called *Real Women* is about the lives and relationships of five former school friends. In this show, family, husbands, and work are all less important than friendships. One of its actresses says the show reflects her own experience. "Friendship is about commitment and loyalty. I don't see some of my friends for ages but when we get together, it is as if time hasn't passed."

5 This is true of Erika and Jane's friendship. With Erika's family 200 miles away, it is Jane who keeps a spare set of keys to Erika's apartment and waters her plants whenever she is away. "Having Jane around gives me a certain amount of freedom. It is not the kind of thing that you could ask anyone to do, but she knows I would do the same for her." Erika feels that because she no longer sees her family every day, she now enjoys a closer relationship with her best friend. Jane, who may move to a different city soon, is worried about leaving such a support system of friends. "My friends have more to do with my life than my parents and, therefore, I don't have to spend a lot of time explaining things to them. Friends are more up to date with what is happening."

Adapted from *The Independent*.

READING TIP
Always pay attention to pronouns — like *it, this*, and *which*. They are important for understanding the meaning of the text. For example, *it* in the first sentence means "the person calling late at night."

Before you read

Thinking about personal experience

Complete the sentences so that they are true about you. Write *friend* or *family member* in each blank.

1. Someone calls you late at night. The person is probably a _____.

2. You don't see someone for ages but when you get together, it is as if time hasn't passed. The person is probably a _____.

3. Someone has a spare set of keys to your apartment and waters your plants whenever you are away. The person is probably a _____.

4. This person is up to date with what is happening in your life. You don't have to spend time explaining things to him or her. The person is probably a _____.

Reading

Scanning

Scan the text to compare what you wrote with the text. Then read the whole text.

After you read

Understanding reference words

A | What do these words refer to?

1. *it* (par. 1, line 2)   <u>The person calling late at night</u>

2. *this* (par. 3, line 7)   _____

3. *its* (par. 4, line 7)   _____

4. *her* (par. 5, line 5)   _____

5. *she* (par. 5, line 6)   _____

6. *them* (par. 5, line 23)   _____

Understanding details

B | Circle the answer that is *not* true.

1. Friends are becoming more important because
   a. people often do not live near their families.
   b. people do not get along with their families.
   c. many marriages end in divorce.

2. For some people, friends have become more important than family because
   a. friends need to be together all the time.
   b. friends are there when these people need help.
   c. friends can talk about anything.

3. Good friends
   a. see each other after a long time and are still friends.
   b. become like family in many ways.
   c. do not always have to tell each other the truth.

Relating reading to personal experience

C | Answer these questions.

1. How would the text be different if it talked about men rather than women?
2. Are friends more important than family in your country? Why or why not?
3. What are some things that you can only ask a friend to do for you? What things can you only ask of family?

Vocabulary expansion

A Complete the chart with the missing words.

Adjective	Noun	Verb
1. *advisable*	advice	advise
2.	confidence	confide
3. consistent	consistency	
4. critical		criticize
5.	dependence	depend
6.	imitation	imitate
7.	judgment	judge
8. supportive	support	

B Read the sentences. Write the parts of speech of the missing words. Then complete the sentences with the correct words from the chart.

1. I ____advise____ you to be friendlier if you want to have more friends.
   verb

2. Be _____ in your dealings with friends instead of being friendly one day and distant the next.

3. A true friend doesn't _____ what you do or criticize you too much.

4. Don't _____ exactly what she does, but try to be a little bit like her.

5. Good friends understand when you have problems. You don't have to _____ anything to them.

6. My parents often _____ what I do. My father doesn't like my clothes, and my mother doesn't like my hair.

7. A _____ friend will always do as he or she promises.

8. She needs to give her family financial _____ during these difficult times.

9. My friend, Tony, is _____. He believes he can succeed at anything.

Friendship and you

Work in pairs. Make a list of DOs and DON'Ts people should follow to keep their friends. Then show others your list.

UNIT 13 Gifts

You are going to read three texts about gifts. First, answer the questions in the boxes.

READING 1

Gift giving

When do people give gifts? What is happening when people give gifts? Find out the answers to these and other questions.

1. When do people in your country give gifts: birthdays? naming ceremonies? weddings? anniversaries? holidays?

2. Who do you most often give gifts to? Who most often gives you gifts?

READING 2

Modern day self-sacrifice

What is the connection between making a sacrifice and giving a gift? This letter from a listener of a radio program explains.

1. How do you usually decide what to get for someone as a gift?

2. What is the most special gift you have given someone? Who did you give it to? Why was it so special?

READING 3

Gifts for the hard to please

Do you ever have trouble finding the right gift for friends or relatives? Here are some gift ideas from a popular store.

1. What's the most unusual gift you have ever received?

2. Do you know someone who is very difficult to buy gifts for? Why is shopping for this person so hard?

Vocabulary

Find out the meanings of the words in *italics*. Then check (✔) the statements that are true about you.

_____ 1. I only give gifts on special *occasions*.

_____ 2. *Recipients* of my gifts are always happy with them.

_____ 3. *Exchanging* gifts is a very important *custom* in my country.

_____ 4. I always *appreciate* the gifts people give me.

_____ 5. If someone gives me a gift, I feel an *obligation* to give something in return.

_____ 6. I don't like receiving an *extravagant* gift.

Gift giving

1   There are many occasions for giving gifts in modern industrialized societies: birthdays, naming ceremonies, weddings, anniversaries, New Year. It is common to give gifts on many of these celebrations in western cultures. In addition, special events, such as one's first day of school or graduation from university, often require gift giving.

2   What is happening when we give gifts? Most important, we are *exchanging* gifts. If someone gives me a gift for my birthday, I know that I am usually expected to give one on his or her next birthday. A gift establishes or confirms a social obligation.

3   Gifts cement personal relationships and provide a means of communication between loved ones. People say that a gift lets the recipient know we are thinking of them, that we want to make the person "feel special." We want people to feel wanted, to feel part of our social or family group. We give presents to say "I'm sorry." Sometimes we try hard to find a present that someone will like. Sometimes we give things that we like or would feel comfortable with. In all these cases, the gifts are sending out messages — often very eloquent ones.

4   People tend to talk about presents in a rather mystical way. A woman whose mother had died years ago described the many gifts around her house. These were gifts that her mother had given her over the years: "I appreciate these, and they mean something to me," the woman said, "because I remember the occasion they were given on, and that it was from my mother, and the relationship we've had." The gifts remain and keep the memory of the relationship alive. This woman felt the same way about the gifts she gave to others. She hoped that the recipients would look at her gifts in years to come and remember her.

5   Emotions like these reveal that a positive spirit still lies behind gift giving. They prove that the anthropologist Claude Lévi-Strauss was wrong to say that modern western gift giving is highly wasteful. Studies in Canada and elsewhere have also shown that this is not the case. Gifts are not usually duplicated when so many presents are given. The emotional benefit for the participants in the gift exchange is reason alone for the tradition to continue.

Adapted from *A Celebration of Customs and Rituals.*

Before you read

Look at these sentences from the text. Then check (✔) the title of the book below that you think the text is from.

There are many occasions for giving gifts in modern industrialized societies.
What is happening when we give gifts?
People tend to talk about presents in a rather mystical way.

_____ 1. *What Should I Bring? Great Gift Ideas for Every Occasion*

_____ 2. *The Commercialism of Gift Giving in America*

_____ 3. *A Celebration of Customs and Rituals*

Reading

Scan the text to check your prediction. Then read the whole text.

After you read

A | **Write the number of each paragraph next to its main idea.**

__4__ a. This paragraph gives a specific example of why gift giving is important to people.

_____ b. This paragraph suggests that those who have a negative opinion of gift giving are wrong.

_____ c. This paragraph specifies occasions when people give gifts.

_____ d. This paragraph discusses the social obligation of gift giving.

_____ e. This paragraph explains some reasons why people give gifts.

B | **Find the words in *italics* in the reading. Circle the meaning of each word.**

1. *cement* (par. 3)   a. make something stronger
                          b. make something less important

2. *eloquent* (par. 3)   a. difficult to understand
                          b. well-expressed

3. *mystical* (par. 4)   a. funny
                          b. religious or spiritual

4. *wasteful* (par. 5)   a. spending money on things you don't need
                          b. throwing away things you don't need

5. *duplicated* (par. 5) a. repeated
                          b. planned

C | **Answer these questions.**

1. When was the last time you gave someone a gift? What was the occasion?
2. What was the last gift you received? Who was it from? What was your reaction?
3. Do you think that there are any negative aspects of gift giving? For example, do you think it is wasteful?

Modern day self-sacrifice

Dear Dr. Laura,

1 I just heard you tell an old story of gift giving and unselfish love. You doubted that such unselfish love would happen in today's world. Well, I'm here to give you hope.

2 I wanted to do something very special for my fifteen-year-old son, who has always been the perfect child. He worked all summer to earn enough money to buy a used dirt motorcycle. Then, he spent hours and hours restoring it until it looked almost new.

3 I was so proud of him that I bought him the shiniest helmet and a riding outfit.

4 I could hardly wait for him to open up his gift. In fact, I barely slept the night before.

5 Upon awakening, I went into the kitchen to start the coffee, tea, and morning goodies. In the living room was a beautiful keyboard with a big red bow and a note: "To my wonderful mother, all my love, your son."

6 I was so astonished. It had been a long-standing joke in our household that I wanted a piano so that I could take lessons. My husband's response was "learn to play the piano, and I'll get you one."

7 I stood there shocked, crying a river, asking myself how my son could afford this extravagant gift.

8 Of course, the house awoke, and my son was thrilled with my reaction. Many hugs and kisses were exchanged, and I immediately wanted him to open my special gift.

9 As he saw the helmet and outfit, the look on his face was not exactly what I was expecting. Then it dawned on me. He had sold the motorcycle to get me the keyboard.

10 Of course I was the proudest mother ever on that day, and my feet never hit the ground for a month.

11 So I wanted you to know, that kind of love still exists and lives even in the ever-changing world of me, me, me!

12 Thought you'd love to share this story.

13 P.S. The next day, my husband and I bought him a new "used" already shiny motorcycle.

Adapted from www.drlaura.com/letters/

Before you read

Look at these words and phrases from the text. What do you think happens in the story?

son
dirt motorcycle
helmet and riding outfit
a beautiful keyboard

"To my wonderful mother"
wanted a piano
many hugs and kisses
the proudest mother

Reading

Scan the text to check your prediction. Then read the whole text.

After you read

A Number the sentences from 1 (first event) to 7 (last event).

_____ a. The writer and her husband bought their son a motorcycle.

_____ b. The writer's son spent a lot of time making his motorcycle look new.

_____ c. The writer realized that her son no longer had his motorcycle.

_____ d. The writer gave her son a motorcycle helmet and riding outfit as a gift.

_____ e. The writer's son gave his mother a keyboard as a gift.

__1__ f. The writer's son bought a dirt motorcycle.

_____ g. The writer's son was not as happy with the gift as his mother expected.

B Circle the correct answers.

1. I stood there shocked, crying a river. (par. 7)
   a. I was so shocked that I sat down near a river and cried.
   b. I was so shocked that I cried a lot.
2. . . . my feet never hit the ground for a month. (par. 10)
   a. I ran a lot for a month.
   b. I was very, very happy.
3. . . . love still exists and lives even in the ever-changing world . . . (par. 11)
   a. The world changes, but unselfish love still exists, as it did before.
   b. We live and love in a world that never changes.
4. . . . world of me, me, me! (par. 11)
   a. A world where people think of themselves first.
   b. A world where people think of others before they think of themselves.
5. . . . I bought him a new "used" already shiny motorcycle. (par. 13)
   a. We got him a motorcycle that was shiny because it was new.
   b. We got him a motorcycle that wasn't new, but it was in good condition.

C Answer these questions.

1. What examples of unselfish giving do you know?
2. Think of two people you know. What is the most special gift they could get?
3. What sacrifices have you made in your life to help other people?

Gifts for the **hard** to please

Travel with an alarm clock, weather-trend indicator, smoke detector, motion sensor, and bedside flashlight— all in one.

***Talking* Travel Companion®**

1   Feel safer in any hotel room anywhere in the world. Our *Talking* Travel Companion® separates into two multifunctional devices: The first is a combination flashlight, barometric weather-trend indicator, and alarm clock. Press a button, and a pleasant voice announces the time and weather trend — improving, steady, or worsening. Its flip-up LCD screen shows time, room temperature in Fahrenheit or Celsius, calendar, and weather trend. The four-step alarm wakes you gradually with the sound of church bells. The "super-snooze" feature allows you to add 10, 20, or 30 additional minutes of sleep.

2   The second device is a combination motion sensor/smoke detector. Hang it from a door, a window, a piece of luggage — anything you don't want moved — and if disturbed, it sounds a loud alarm. If it detects smoke, a separate alarm will alert you. Its small size and light weight allow it to run on one 9v and 4 AAA batteries (order separately). One-year warranty. Created by Sharper Image Design.

Enjoy an enchanting night-light with an ever-changing spectrum of color.

Color Flow™ Light Show

3   With the Color Flow™ Light Show night-light you'll experience an ever-changing spectrum of beautiful color from three LED lights—blue,

red, and green — using blending technology that slowly melts and mixes colors. There's never a need to change a bulb or a lens! Leave Color Flow™ Light Show running in a darkened room and drift away, bathed in rose, red, pink, aqua, teal, blue and violet light. If a certain mix strikes your fancy, press the Color Lock button to enjoy it as long as you like. Plugs into wall outlet. One-year warranty. Created by Sharper Image Design.

Wear your own climate-control system — stay warm in winter, cool in summer.

Personal Warm + Cool System™

4   Our Personal Warm+Cool System™ fits comfortably around your neck and delivers hours of comfort. This electronic device is trim, discreet, and ultra lightweight. Turn the dial to "warm" and within seconds your entire body feels warmer. Or turn the dial to "cool" and enjoy your own "personal air conditioner" on the hottest, most humid days. Runs on 3 C batteries (not included) in a small included battery pack that hides in a pocket or on a belt. One-year warranty. Select small or large. Created by Sharper Image Design.

> **READING TIP**
> Sometimes you can guess the meaning of a new word by looking at the pictures in the text. For example, the picture of the *Talking* Travel Companion® shows what an "LCD screen" is.

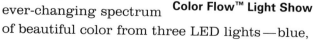

Adapted from *The New Millennium 2001 Sharper Image Catalog.*

Before you read

Look at the pictures and headings on the opposite page. Then check (✔) the column of the product you think each phrase describes.

	Talking Travel Companion®	Color Flow™ Light Show	Personal Warm+ Cool System™
1. a certain mix strikes your fancy			
2. change a bulb or a lens			
3. church bells			
4. a darkened room			
5. flip-up LCD screen			
6. the hottest, most humid days			
7. a loud alarm			
8. melts and mixes colors			
9. "super-snooze" feature			
10. trim, discreet, and ultra lightweight			

Reading

Scan the text to check your predictions. Then read the whole text.

After you read

A Where does the text probably come from? Check (✔) the correct answer.

_____ 1. an instruction manual   _____ 3. a catalog

_____ 2. a textbook   _____ 4. an encyclopedia

B Answer the questions. Write *not given* if the text does not give the information.

1. Where will the *Talking* Travel Companion® be useful?   *in a hotel room*
2. Where can the Color Flow™ Light Show be used?   _____
3. How do you use the Personal Warm+Cool System™?   _____
4. Where is the *Talking* Travel Companion® made?   _____
5. Which products use batteries?   _____
6. How much does the Color Flow™ Light Show weigh?   _____
7. How big is the Personal Warm+Cool System™?   _____
8. Where do you put the Personal Warm+Cool System™?   _____

C Answer these questions.

1. Who do you know that would like the *Talking* Travel Companion®? the Color Flow™ Light Show? the Personal Warm+Cool System™?
2. Would you be interested in finding out about other products this company makes? Why or why not?
3. Where is the best place you know to find gifts for people who are hard to please?

Vocabulary expansion

Skim the dictionary entries. Then find the correct definition for each word in italics in the sentences below.

1. **present** /ˈprez·ənt/ *n* [C] something that is given without being asked for, esp. on a special occasion, to show friendship, or to say thank you; a GIFT • *Did you wrap the present?*
2. **present** /ˈprez·ənt/ *n* [U] this period of time, not the past or the future; now • *The story moves back and forth between the past and the present.*
3. **present** /ˈprez·ənt/ *adj* [not gradable] in a particular place • *The mayor was present during the entire meeting.*

4. **use** /juːz/ *v* [T] to reduce (the amount of something) • *We have used all the funds in that account.*
5. **use** /juːz/ *v* [T] to be friendly toward (someone) for your own advantage or purposes • *She used him to help her get into movies and then discarded him.*
6. **used** /juːzd/ *adj* [not gradable] already owned or put to a purpose by someone else; not new • *We're looking for a used car in good condition.*

7. **run** /rʌn/ *v* [I/T] to move your legs faster than when walking, with the weight of your body pressing forward • *He runs five miles a day.*
8. **run** /rʌn/ *v* [I/T] to travel or go, to move (something), or to be positioned in a particular way • *I'm going to run down to the bank to cash my check.*
9. **run** /rʌn/ *v* [I/T] to manage or operate (something), esp. in a particular way • *If something runs on a particular type of energy, it uses that type of energy to operate.*
10. **run** /rʌn/ *v* [I/T] to cause (a liquid) to flow, or to produce a liquid that flows • *He ran a little cold water into the sink.*

11. **state** /steit/ *n* [C] a condition or way of being • *The stable was preserved in its original state.*
12. **state** /steit/ *n* [C] one of the political units that some countries, such as the US, are divided into • *New York State*
13. **state** /steit/ *v* [T] to express (information), esp. clearly and carefully • *His will states the property is to be sold.*

___3___ a. I was *present* when she opened her gifts.

_____ b. I have no plans at *present* to go to the birthday party, so I don't need to buy anything.

_____ c. I prefer something inexpensive to something *used*.

_____ d. I *used* all the money I had to buy that gift.

_____ e. You *used* me just because you wanted me to buy you something expensive.

_____ f. She was so happy when she opened the gift that tears were *running* down her face.

_____ g. Can I use your car to *run* to the store and pick up a present?

_____ h. Can you just *state* what you want me to get you? You never like what I buy!

_____ i. The package arrived in such a bad *state* that I didn't keep it.

Gifts and you

With a partner, make a list of the best gifts to give to everyone in your class (including your teacher!). Then tell the class the gifts you have chosen for them.

UNIT 14 Emotions

You are going to read three texts about emotions. First, answer the questions in the boxes.

READING 1

Jokes can't always make you laugh

Do you have a good sense of humor? This website explains what a sense of humor is and why laughter is so important.

1. Why are some people better than others at telling jokes? Are you good at telling jokes?
2. What makes you laugh?

READING 2

Envy: Is it hurting or helping you?

People are often envious of others. In this article you will learn the causes of envy and how to deal with it.

1. What are some things people typically envy?
2. What do you think causes envy? Are some people more likely to be envious than others?

READING 3

The value of tears

This magazine article explains why we cry and why crying is not necessarily something to be ashamed of.

1. Do you cry easily? What causes you to cry? How do you feel after you cry?
2. Do you feel embarrassed when you cry in public? Why or why not?

Vocabulary

Find out the meanings of the words in the box. Then mark each word as noun (*N*) or adjective (*A*), and answer the questions.

anger	envy	insecure	resentment	tense
angry	fear	jealous	shock	tension
embarrassed	frustrated	lonely	stress	upset
envious	grief	powerless	stressed	

1. Which of these emotions make you feel the worst?
2. Which of these emotions might make you a stronger person?

Jokes can't always make you laugh

1 As awareness of the benefits of humor and laughter increases, most of us want to get all the laughs we can. It seems that almost every day there is another news bulletin about the power of humor and laughter to heal us physically, mentally, emotionally, and spiritually. Every system of the body responds to laughter in some important, positive, or healing way.

Sense of humor

2 Many people mistakenly believe that you are born with a sense of humor. They think that when it comes to a sense of humor, "either you've got it or you don't." This is false! What is true, however, is that the capacity to laugh and smile is virtually inborn.

3 The parts of the brain and central nervous system that control laughing and smiling are mature at birth in human infants, but that is not the same thing as having a sense of humor. (After all, when an infant laughs in its crib we don't rush over and say, "That kid has a great sense of humor!") Your sense of humor is something you can develop over a lifetime. Lose your inhibitions and try to laugh at yourself — then you will make others laugh too.

Jokes are not everything

4 Humor includes a lot more than laughing and joke telling. Many people worry needlessly that they do not have a good sense of humor because they are not good joke tellers. More than jokes, a sense of humor requires being willing and able to see the funny side of life's situations as they happen. In fact, one of the best definitions of a sense of humor is "the ability to see the nonserious element in a situation." The ability to tell jokes is only one small part of humor.

5 There may be a thousand different ways to express your sense of humor, and joke telling is only one of those ways. Some people take the time to memorize jokes, and they may even have good timing and delivery. However, if they cannot see the humor when there is a foul-up or setback in everyday life, then they don't really have a very good sense of humor.

Adapted from *www.LaughterClubs.com.*

Before you read

Relating to the topic

Circle the information you agree with.

1. Laughter is
   a. good for your health.
   b. bad for your health.
2. A sense of humor is
   a. something we are born with.
   b. something we develop.
3. The ability to tell jokes is
   a. the most important part of humor.
   b. only a small part of humor.

4. A sense of humor requires
   a. the ability to tell jokes.
   b. the ability to see the funny side of life.
5. A good joke teller
   a. has good timing and delivery.
   b. always sees the funny side of life.

Reading

Scanning

Scan the text to find out which statements the writer agrees with. Then read the whole text.

After you read

Guessing meaning from context

A **Find the words in *italics* in the reading. Circle the meaning of each word.**

1. *heal* (par. 1)
   a. make sick
   b. make well after an illness
2. *mature* (par. 3)
   a. not existing yet
   b. fully developed
3. *inhibitions* (par. 3)
   a. lack of confidence to act naturally
   b. desire to show people who you are

4. *willing* (par. 4)
   a. ready to do something
   b. not ready to do something
5. *foul-up* (par. 5)
   a. something that goes well
   b. something that doesn't go well
6. *setback* (par. 5)
   a. something that helps you
   b. something that causes problems

Understanding details

B **Answer the questions.**

1. How are humor and laughter good for people?
   Humor and laughter can heal us physically, mentally, emotionally, and spiritually.
2. What aspect of humor is inborn? Why is this so?

   _____

3. What can people do in order to develop their sense of humor?

   _____

4. Why do many people think they do not have a good sense of humor?

   _____

5. What is the writer's definition of a sense of humor?

   _____

Relating reading to personal experience

C **Answer these questions.**

1. Do you think that you have a good sense of humor? How do you know?
2. Who makes you laugh? What makes them so funny?
3. What is your favorite joke?

Envy: Is it hurting or helping you?

1   "Sometimes I'm so envious of my friends, I hate them," says Kimberly. "I was at dinner a month ago, celebrating a friend's engagement, and I blurted out that 50 percent of marriages end in divorce. I was frustrated about not being in a serious relationship myself. My envy took over, and I became a different person."

2   Kimberly was experiencing envy — the desire for what someone else has and resentment of that person for having it. However, this doesn't mean she is a bad person. "Everyone experiences envy — it's a normal human emotion," explains psychologist Karen Peterson.

3   Envy doesn't have to make us feel powerless and bad about ourselves. Here are some ways to deal with envy and turn the bad into the good.

4   Kimberly's envy at her friend's engagement caused her to make the unkind remark about divorce. When you feel you want to express your envy in a negative way, stop it. Instead, think about what it is you're envious of. "When she announced her engagement, it made me feel lonely and insecure," admits Kimberly. Once you figure out why you're envious, it's much easier to eventually grow from the experience. "Envy can be an excellent educator," states Peterson, "as long as you are open to learning its lessons."

5   Lucy and her friend were both trying to get a better position at their company. Lucy thought she would get the promotion, but things didn't work out that way. Instead, her friend got the promotion, and Lucy became upset and jealous. Full of envy, she started saying hurtful things about her friend. "That wasn't like me, but I couldn't think straight," she explains. She said mean things about her

friend because not getting the job made her feel bad about herself, explains Peterson. Her reaction didn't make her feel better, though; it just strengthened her negative feelings. Peterson says it would be better to try to understand why your friend got the promotion and learn from that instead of having negative feelings.

6   If you feel that getting what you want — marriage or lots of money — is impossible, remember that every big goal is made up of thousands of tiny steps. "Think of one or two small things you could do each week to help you come closer to your ultimate goal, then do them," advises author Doreen Virtue. After Kimberly left her friend's party feeling guilty about her nasty comment, she decided to make some changes in her social life. Making that decision was the first step in getting rid of envy.

READING TIP

Understanding punctuation can help you understand the meaning of a text. Dashes (—) can be used to give definitions and explanations. Some examples are ". . . envy — the desire for what someone else has" and ". . . what you want — marriage or lots of money — is . . ."

Adapted from *Cosmopolitan*.

Before you read

Look at the title of the reading on the opposite page. Then check (✔) the information you think you will read about in the text.

_____ 1. a definition of envy

_____ 2. stories about people who have felt envy

_____ 3. reasons people feel envy

_____ 4. advice on how to deal with envy

_____ 5. results of a survey that asked people about envy

Reading

Scan the text to check your predictions. Then read the whole text.

After you read

A Where does the text probably come from? Check (✔) the correct answer.

_____ 1. a women's magazine

_____ 2. the front page of a newspaper

_____ 3. a psychology textbook

B What do these words refer to? Circle the correct answer.

1. *them* (par. 1, line 2)   a. people   (b.) friends
2. *this* (par. 2, line 3)   a. envy   b. desire
3. *it* (par. 4, line 4)   a. the unkind remark   b. the feeling of wanting to express envy
4. *its* (par. 4, line 12)   a. an excellent educator's   b. envy's
5. *that* (par. 5, line 16) a. why your friend got the promotion   b. your friend
6. *them* (par. 6, line 7)   a. one or two small things   b. tiny steps

C The sentences below are false. Change one word in each sentence to make it true.

1. It is ~~not~~ *perfectly* normal to feel envy.
2. Envy is something that some people feel.
3. Envy can teach you a lot about others.
4. Envy makes you feel good about yourself.
5. When you feel envy, you should ask yourself where you are feeling it.
6. If you want to get rid of your envy, set goals that seem impossible to achieve.

D Answer these questions.

1. Do you think that envy is different for men and women? If so, how?
2. What advice would you give to someone who is envious of a friend who:
   a. gets a promotion at work?   b. always looks good?   c. gets a lot of invitations?
3. Have you been envious of anyone lately? How did it make you feel about yourself?

The value of tears

They can conquer stress and make you feel better . . . so go ahead, cry.

1 Tears can ruin make-up, bring conversation to a stop, and give you a runny nose. They leave you embarrassed and without energy. Still, crying is a fact of life, and your tears are very useful. Even when you're not crying, they make a film over the eye's surface. This film contains a substance that protects your eyes against infection.

2 When tears fall, they relieve stress; but we tend to fight them for all sorts of reasons. "People worry about showing their emotions, afraid that once they lose control they'll never get it back," explains psychologist Dorothy Rowe. "As children we might have been punished for shedding tears or expressing anger; as adults we still fear the consequences of showing emotions. The fact is, no emotion lasts forever." After we cry, the feelings that caused the tears often disappear.

3 Almost any emotion — good or bad, happy or sad — can bring on tears. Crying is an escape mechanism for built-up emotions. Tears help you when you feel you are ready to explode because of very strong feelings. How many times have you laughed until you cried? That is an example of how tears release feelings. This may explain why men, who are usually afraid to cry, suffer more heart attacks than women. Women cry. Men explode.

4 Sometimes people become very stressed and can't cry. Whatever emotion they are feeling — shock, anger, fear, or grief — is being held back.

5 "Everyone has the need to cry," says psychotherapist Vera Diamond. She explains that therapy often consists of giving people permission to cry. She even gives crying exercises, in which patients practice crying just to become used to expressing emotion. She suggests safe, private places to cry, like under the bedcovers or in the car. Crying is a way of relieving tension, but people don't like it when others cry because it makes them tense. They too may be holding back a need to cry, and they'll do just about anything to make you stop.

6 In certain situations, such as at work, tears are not appropriate. It's good not to cry during a tense business discussion. "But once you are safely behind closed doors, don't just cry," Diamond says. She suggests that you act out the whole situation again and be as noisy and angry as you like. It will help you feel better. "And," she adds, "once your tears have released the stress, you can begin to think of logical ways to deal with the problem."

7 Tears are a sign of our ability to feel. If you find yourself near someone crying, deal with it. And never be afraid to cry yourself.

Adapted from *Redbook*.

Before you read

How much do you know about crying? Mark each statement true (*T*) or false (*F*).

_____ 1. Crying is good for people's eyes and their health.

_____ 2. Crying relieves stress.

_____ 3. Only sad things make people cry.

_____ 4. Too much stress can make it difficult for people to cry.

_____ 5. Tears are a natural way for people to release their emotions.

Reading

Scan the text to check your answers. Then read the whole text.

After you read

A Check (✔) the statement that best expresses the main idea of the text. Then write the
paragraph number next to the main idea of that paragraph.

_3_ a. People's emotions cause them to cry.

_____ b. Crying is natural and is good for you.

_____ c. What should you do when you want to cry but you shouldn't?

_____ d. There are reasons why people don't like to cry.

_____ e. There are some things people can do if it is difficult for them to cry.

B Check (✔) the correct column.

	Inference	Restatement	Not in the text
1. Pain can cause people to cry.			✓
2. Parents should not teach their children that it is bad to cry.			
3. People are afraid of crying because it shows they have no control.			
4. Sad movies can cause people to cry.			
5. It is good for people to cry.			
6. Each eye produces tears every minute.			
7. Therapy can help people who have difficulty crying.			
8. If you're with someone who is crying, you shouldn't stop them from crying.			

C Answer these questions.

1. In your experience, do men cry less than women? If so, why?
2. Are you uncomfortable when someone around you cries? What do you do?
3. Should people who can't cry see a therapist? Why or why not?

Vocabulary expansion

A How do the people in the pictures feel? Write a sentence using the adjectives below.

1.

The students are very bored.

2.

3.

4.

5.

6.

Feelings		Qualities of people, things, and situations	
I feel . . .		_It is . . ._	
bored	frustrated	boring	frustrating
embarrassed	interested	embarrassing	interesting
excited	tired	exciting	tiring

B What's your opinion of these situations and things? Use adjectives with _-ing_ endings to describe each activity.

1. a three-hour exam _A three-hour exam is really tiring. I usually have a headache at the end._

2. a soccer game _____

3. a museum _____

4. shopping _____

5. speaking a foreign language _____

6. movies about famous events _____

Emotions and you

Imagine someone feeling intense envy, anger, or joy. Choose one of these emotions.
Then make up a story about what happened to the person to cause such strong emotions.

15 Food

You are going to read three texts about food. First, answer the questions in the boxes.

READING 1

Chocolate

Do you know how to tell the quality of chocolate? Do you believe that chocolate is bad for you? Learn the truth about this popular treat.

1. Do you like to eat chocolate? Why or why not?
2. What is the best place to buy good quality chocolate in your country? Which company do you think makes the best chocolate?

READING 2

What our taste buds say about us

This newspaper article presents some recent research on why people prefer certain foods to others.

1. What food do you most like to eat?
2. Will you eat anything? Are there certain kinds of food you won't eat?

READING 3

It tastes just like chicken

Your host puts a plate of strange-looking food in front of you. What should you do? Read this excerpt from a book for some advice.

1. Besides food from your country, what other types of food do you like?
2. What do you think people should do when they don't like the food their host gives them?

Vocabulary

Find out the meanings of the words in the box. Then write each word under the correct heading.

aroma	chew	salty	smell	swallow
bitter	flavor	slice	sour	texture

WHAT PEOPLE DO WITH FOOD	HOW FOOD TASTES	HOW PEOPLE JUDGE FOOD

Chocolate

Assessing quality

1   We use all our senses — sight, smell, sound, touch, and taste — when we assess the quality of dark chocolate.

2   **Appearance:** The chocolate should be smooth, very shiny, and pure mahogany in color.

3   **Smell:** The chocolate should not smell too sweet.

4   **Sound:** The chocolate should be crisp and make a distinct "snap" when broken in two.

5   **Touch:** Chocolate with a high cacao butter content should quickly start to melt when held in the hand — this is a good sign. In the mouth, it should feel ultra smooth, and it should melt instantly.

6   **Taste:** Chocolate contains a great variety of flavors and aromas that continue to develop in the mouth. The basic flavors are bitterness with a hint of acidity, sweetness with a suggestion of sourness, and just a touch of saltiness to help release the aromas of cocoa, pineapple, banana, vanilla, and cinnamon.

Tasting techniques

7   It is best to taste chocolate on an empty stomach. It is also best to eat it at room temperature.

8   Allow the chocolate to sit in your mouth for a few moments to release its primary flavors and aromas. Then chew it five to ten times to release the secondary aromas. Let it rest lightly against the roof of your mouth to experience the full range of flavors. Finally, enjoy the lingering tastes in your mouth.

Myths and prejudices

9   Claims that chocolate is bad for you are almost certainly based on the added sugar and vegetable fat in poor quality chocolate. Quality chocolate contains pure cacao butter with no added fat and little sugar — in some cases hardly any. Several medical experts have also disputed claims that chocolate causes migraines, obesity, acne, and tooth decay.

10   **Migraines:** People have thought that cheese and chocolate cause migraines, which can be set off by large doses of tyramine, a normal substance in the body. Chocolate, however, contains only a very small quantity of tyramine, far less than cheese.

11   **Obesity:** Good quality dark chocolate is unlikely to be the cause of obesity because it contains far less sugar than poor quality chocolate. Furthermore, because it is more expensive, people are less likely to eat good quality chocolate in large quantities.

12   **Acne:** American surveys show no relationship between chocolate and acne in teenagers. More likely causes are hormonal imbalances and a lack of fresh fruit and vegetables in the diet.

13   **Tooth decay:** Chocolate melts in the mouth and is therefore in contact with the teeth for a relatively short time.

Adapted from *The Cook's Encyclopedia of Chocolate.*

Before you read

How much do you know about chocolate? Mark each statement true (*T*) or false (*F*).

_____ 1. Chocolate causes acne.

_____ 2. Chocolate should look smooth and shiny.

_____ 3. Chocolate causes tooth decay.

_____ 4. Chocolate causes migraines.

_____ 5. Chocolate should start to melt when you hold it in your hand.

_____ 6. Chocolate causes obesity.

Reading

Scan the text to check your answers. Then read the whole text.

After you read

A Match each statement with the part of the text the person should read.

_____ 1. Jennifer loves chocolate. However, she tries not to eat too much of it because she thinks it's bad for her.

_____ 2. Matthew wants to learn how to appreciate chocolate more when he eats it.

_____ 3. Emily has five different kinds of chocolate and wants to know which is the best.

a. Assessing quality

b. Tasting techniques

c. Myths and prejudices

B Check (✔) the correct statement.

_____ 1. The writer thinks chocolate is bad for you.

_____ 2. The writer prefers low-quality chocolate.

_____ 3. The writer knows a lot about chocolate.

C Mark each statement *the speaker knows a lot about chocolate* (✔) or *the speaker does not know a lot about chocolate* (X).

_X_ 1. "It doesn't matter how chocolate looks or smells. Taste is the important thing."

_____ 2. "Let's have some chocolate for dessert."

_____ 3. "This is good quality chocolate. It won't make you fat."

_____ 4. "My son has a skin problem because he eats too much chocolate."

_____ 5. "This chocolate isn't any good. It's melting too quickly."

_____ 6. "Listen. I'm going to break the chocolate. If it's good, we'll hear it!"

_____ 7. "Let's have some chocolate now. I'll get it out of the refrigerator."

D Answer these questions.

1. After reading the text, will you eat chocolate more often? Why or why not?
2. What other foods or drinks cause migraines, obesity, acne, or tooth decay?
3. Think of something you like to eat or drink. How do you judge its quality?

What our taste buds say about us

1 Mothers have known it for years. Give the children a hamburger, and they will love it; spend hours making a home-cooked meal, and they will leave it on the plate. Now French scientists have discovered why. According to researchers near Paris, the brain does not respond well to un-familiar tastes. Sensations are not as strong when the mind is struggling to understand messages that come from the tongue. This provides little reason to taste new things.

2 According to Annick Faurion, a researcher at a French laboratory, "Human beings, like rats, are naturally neophobic — we are afraid of anything new. If you give rats some food that they have never had before, they will turn their backs on it out of fear. We are the same. It is possible to introduce new foods, but only in the right psychological context, like a birthday. Once the introduction has been made, the fact of having a full stomach is physically pleasing, so the next time it is easier." Faurion admitted, however, that some foods are more tempting than others. Scientists are sure that we are born with a sweet tooth. This is why young children have a natural desire for sugar.

3 Another discovery Faurion made is how a sense of smell affects the taste buds. In one experiment, chemical substances were put on the tongues of human participants. At the same time, air was blown down the participants' noses so they could

not smell the chemical substances. Faurion found that no two people got the same sensation from the same food. Physical, psychological, and cultural differences shaped the response.

4 Faurion said the intensity of feelings about food depended upon knowledge of it. The average student who eats a new dish will have only a cloudy image of it, but gastronomes will have an exciting experience. Their tongues are trained to appreciate fine differences, much like someone who has a great musical ear. "This is why someone who eats hamburgers every day likes them and becomes a hamburger connoisseur," Faurion said. "They really can tell the difference between a Big Mac and a Burger King, just like the Japanese can tell the difference between varieties of rice that taste the same to Europeans."

5 Faurion's findings are important to the food industry. She said the increase in vacuum-packed and frozen food limits the variety of tastes in western society. This hinders people's ability to appreciate anything else. "There is no reason that industrial food should be so tasteless. It is just that 90 percent of the technicians responsible for these meals doesn't know anything about food. But it is doing great damage."

Adapted from *The Times*.

Thinking about personal experience

Check (✔) the statements you think are true.

_____ 1. People generally don't like to eat food they are unfamiliar with.

_____ 2. The brain plays a role in the food we like and don't like.

_____ 3. For the most part, young children like to eat sugar.

_____ 4. Some people can taste the fine differences in food better than others.

_____ 5. Vacuum-packed and frozen foods do not usually have much taste.

Reading

Scanning

Scan the text to check your answers. Then read the whole text.

After you read

Guessing meaning from context

A Find the words in *italics* in the reading. Then complete the sentences.

a connoisseur (par. 4)   *intensity* (par. 4)   *a sweet tooth* (par. 2)
a gastronome (par. 4)   *a sensation* (par. 1)   *tempting* (par. 2)

1. If you have _a sweet tooth_, you like to eat cookies, candy, chocolate, and cake.

2. _____ is something you experience physically.

3. _____ enjoys food and knows a lot about cooking and restaurants.

4. When you demonstrate _____, you show great seriousness or passion.

5. When food is _____, you want to eat it.

6. _____ knows a lot about something and appreciates good quality.

Understanding details

B Circle the correct answers.

1. Why do children prefer a hamburger to a home-cooked meal?
   a. Children prefer food that is easy to make.
   (b.) The brain doesn't respond well to unfamiliar tastes.

2. When are people willing to try new food?
   a. when they are at a happy occasion
   b. when they have already eaten

3. What causes people to like certain foods but not others?
   a. differences in people — for example, cultural differences
   b. the smell of the food

4. Why can some people appreciate the fine differences in food?
   a. They eat a lot of food.
   b. They know a lot about food.

Relating reading to personal experience

C Answer these questions.

1. Do you think you are a gastronome or someone with ordinary tasting skills?
2. Is it a problem that people are eating more frozen and fast foods? Why or why not?
3. What food did you not eat as a child that you like to eat now? What food did you eat as a child that you don't like to eat now?

It tastes just like chicken

1   Away from home, eating is more than just a way to keep your stomach full. It is a language all its own, and no words can say, "Glad to meet you . . . glad to be doing business with you . . ." quite like sharing a meal offered by your host.

2   Clearly, mealtime is not the time for you to say, "Thanks, but no thanks." Acceptance of the food on your plate means acceptance of host, country, and company. So, no matter how difficult it may be to swallow, swallow. Or, as one experienced traveler says, "Travel with a cast-iron stomach and eat everything everywhere."

3   Often, the food offered is your host country's proudest culinary achievement. What would Americans think of a French person who refused a bite of homemade apple pie or sizzling steak? Our discomfort comes not so much from the thing itself; it comes from our unfamiliarity with it. After all, an oyster has remarkably the same look and consistency as a sheep's eye; and a first look at a lobster would remind almost anybody of a creature from a science fiction movie, not something you dip in melted butter and eat. By the way, in Saudi Arabia sheep's eyes are a delicacy and in parts of China it's bear's paw soup.

4   Can you refuse such food without being rude? Most experienced business travelers say no, at least not before taking at least a few bites. It helps, though, to slice any item very thin. This way, you minimize the texture — gristly, slimy, and so on — and the reminder of where it came from. Or, "Swallow it quickly," as one traveler recommends. "I still can't tell you what sheep's eyeballs taste like." As for dealing with taste, the old line that "it tastes just like chicken" is often thankfully true. Even when the "it" is really rat or snake.

5   Another useful piece of advice is not knowing what you are eating. What's for dinner? Don't ask. Avoid glancing into the kitchen or looking at English-language menus. Your host will be flattered that you are eating the food he offers, and who knows? Maybe it really is chicken in that stew.

READING TIP

Dashes (—   —) around words can indicate that they are examples of the word that comes before. So, *gristly* and *slimy* are examples of different *textures*.

Adapted from *Gestures: The Do's and Taboos of Body Language Around the World.*

Before you read

Thinking about personal experience

Check (✔) the foods you think are common in the United States.

_____ 1. apple pie   _____ 3. oysters   _____ 5. sheep's eyes

_____ 2. steak   _____ 4. lobster   _____ 6. bear's paw soup

Reading

Scanning

Scan the text to check your answers. Then read the whole text.

After you read

Recognizing audience

A Who do you think the text was written for? Check (✔) the correct answer.

_____ 1. people who are going to travel abroad

_____ 2. people who want to cook food from another country

_____ 3. people who are going to teach people from different countries

Recognizing point of view

B What is the nationality of the writer? Check (✔) the correct answer.

_____ 1. Australian   _____ 3. American

_____ 2. Chinese   _____ 4. British

Understanding details

C Check (✔) the information found in the text. For the answers you checked, write a sentence from the text that supports your answer.

✓ 1. why it is impolite not to eat what people in a foreign country offer you
   Acceptance of the food on your plate means acceptance of host, country, and company.

_____ 2. examples of food French people eat

_____

_____ 3. why people are uncomfortable eating food they do not know

_____

_____ 4. advice about what to do when someone offers you food you do not know or like

_____

_____ 5. advice about what to say when someone offers you food you do not know or like

_____

Relating reading to personal experience

D Answer these questions.

1. Which of the foods mentioned in the text would you *not* eat? What would you do if you were offered this food at someone's home?
2. What is your country's "proudest culinary achievement?" How would you feel if a foreign visitor didn't want to try the dish?
3. What food might a foreign visitor to your country find strange?

Vocabulary expansion

A Complete the diagrams with the words from the box. Then add your own word to each diagram.

bake	bitter	boil	~~chew~~	fattening	healthful	~~salty~~	spicy	swallow
bite	bland	broil	delicious	fry	roast	sour	stir-fry	sweet

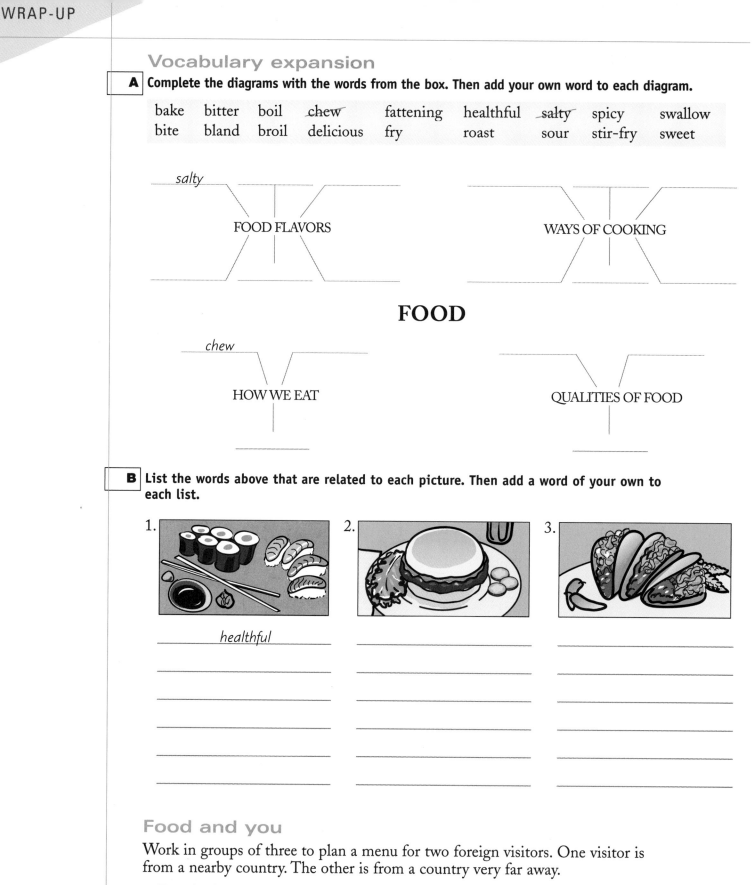

salty

FOOD FLAVORS

WAYS OF COOKING

FOOD

chew

HOW WE EAT

QUALITIES OF FOOD

B List the words above that are related to each picture. Then add a word of your own to each list.

1.

healthful

2.

3.

Food and you

Work in groups of three to plan a menu for two foreign visitors. One visitor is from a nearby country. The other is from a country very far away.

1. Decide the country each comes from.
2. Then decide what to serve each visitor. Are you going to serve them the same meal, or do you think they will like different things?
3. Finally, role play a conversation between the host and the guests. The host should explain the dishes, and the guest should react to the food.

UNIT 16 Sleep & dreams

You are going to read three texts about sleep and dreams. First, answer the questions in the boxes.

READING 1

Power napping is good for the I.Q.

Do you find that you can't think clearly when you don't get enough sleep? This newspaper article reviews research on the connection between sleep and intelligence.

1. How much sleep do you usually get? When do you usually go to bed? When do you usually wake up?
2. Do you ever take naps? If so, how long do you usually sleep? How do you feel after a nap?

READING 2

Common questions about dreams

This website answers some frequently asked questions that people have about dreams.

1. Can you usually remember your dreams? If so, what is a recent dream you remember?
2. What are some things you would like to ask an expert on dreams?

READING 3

What is a dream?

This newspaper article looks at different theories about dreams and their significance.

1. Do you think that your dreams are connected to your waking hours, thoughts, and behavior? Why or why not?
2. Do you think that dreams predict the future? Why or why not?

Vocabulary

Find out the meanings of the words in *italics*. Then check (✔) the statements that are true about you.

_____ 1. Sleep *rejuvenates* me.

_____ 2. Sleep *energizes* me.

_____ 3. A lack of sleep affects my *memory*.

_____ 4. A lack of sleep affects my *alertness*.

_____ 5. Sleep helps me to *function*.

_____ 6. I am a *light sleeper*.

_____ 7. I have *vivid* dreams.

_____ 8. I remember several dreams *nightly*.

Power napping is good for the I.Q.

1 Health professionals increasingly recognize the importance of eight hours' sleep a night. Scientists now believe that sleep is the single most important factor for general health, more important than diet or exercise. Sleep is the only treatment that can claim to restore, rejuvenate, and energize both the body and the brain. The third of our lives that we spend asleep has a profound effect on the two-thirds that we spend awake — affecting our mood, memory, alertness, and performance.

2 Studies show that people in the developed world increasingly spend less time asleep and more time at work or commuting. Dr. Karine Spiegel, at the University of Chicago, has found that the average length of sleep in developed nations has declined from nine hours in 1910 to seven-and-a-half hours today. However, we are biologically ill-equipped to function on little sleep; and losing just one or two hours' sleep a night over a long period of time can have a serious effect on someone's health.

3 According to Canadian scientist Dr. Stanley Coren, every hour of sleep lost in a night also causes us to drop one I.Q. point the next day. In a week of five- or six-hour nights, the average person's I.Q. could drop 15 points; thus, a normally intelligent person starts to have a hard time functioning at all.

4 Most sleep experts agree that humans are designed to sleep for

at least eight hours, but that this should be in two stages: a long sleep at night and a shorter nap in the afternoon. American companies are paying attention to this and are reporting increased levels of alertness in employees who "power nap" at some point during the afternoon, if only for 20 minutes. The argument is that those who are not sleep-deprived are much more efficient at work.

5 The test used to determine sleep deprivation is called the Multiple Sleep Latency Test, or MSLT. In an MSLT, an individual remains in a darkened, quiet room during the day. According to the theory, the more sleep-deprived the individual is, the less time it takes that person to fall asleep. If it takes ten minutes or longer to fall into a light sleep, the participant is probably getting enough sleep; anything less shows moderate sleep deprivation. However, the time of year seems to affect how much sleep an individual requires. People tend to sleep as long as 14 hours in the winter and as little as six hours in summer, without ill effects.

READING TIP To understand a difficult sentence, find the subject. For example, in paragraph 1, what "has a profound effect on the two-thirds that we spend awake"? The answer is "The third of our lives that we spend asleep." That is the subject of the sentence.

Adapted from *The Scotsman.*

Before you read

I.Q. is a person's level of intelligence measured by standardized tests. Check (✔) the statement that you think will be the main idea of the text.

_____ 1. The amount of sleep people get affects their brain function.

_____ 2. People should sleep before they take intelligence tests.

_____ 3. People in power are more intelligent because they take naps.

_____ 4. It is possible to determine if a person gets enough sleep by testing the brain.

Reading

Skim the text to check your prediction. Then read the whole text.

After you read

A **Find the words in *italics* in the reading. Then match each word with its meaning.**

_d_	1. *diet* (par. 1)	a. go down in number
___	2. *treatment* (par. 1)	b. find out facts or information
___	3. *commute* (par. 2)	c. a method of making people feel better
___	4. *decline* (par. 2)	d. what people eat and drink
___	5. *stage* (par. 4)	e. travel to and from work
___	6. *determine* (par. 5)	f. a part of an activity

B **Answer the questions.**

1. How does sleep affect people's everyday life?
   Sleep affects people's mood, memory, alertness, and performance.

2. How does the number of hours people sleep nowadays compare with the number of hours they slept in the past?

3. What is the relationship between the amount of sleep people get and their I.Q.?

4. How many hours should people sleep? When should they sleep?

5. What happens to workers who take a short nap at work?

6. How much sleep do people need at different times of the year?

C **Answer these questions.**

1. How does a lack of sleep affect you?
2. Will you change your sleeping habits after reading this article? Why or why not?
3. What is your ideal sleeping schedule? Why don't you always follow it?

Common questions about dreams

Does everyone dream?

1 Yes. Laboratory studies have shown that we experience our most vivid dreams during a type of sleep called Rapid Eye Movement (REM) sleep. During REM sleep, the brain is very active, the eyes move back and forth rapidly under the lids, and the large muscles of the body are relaxed. REM sleep occurs every 90–100 minutes, three to four times a night, and lasts longer as the night progresses. The final REM period may last as long as 45 minutes. Less vivid dreams occur at other times during the night.

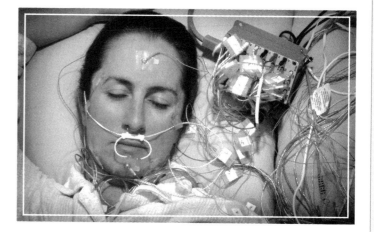

Why do people have trouble remembering their dreams?

2 Some people have no difficulty remembering several dreams nightly. Others recall dreams only occasionally or not at all. By morning, people forget nearly everything that happens throughout the night — including dreams, thoughts that occur, and memories of brief awakening. There is something about sleep that makes it difficult to remember what has occurred, and people forget most dreams unless they write them down. Sometimes they suddenly remember a dream later in the day or on another day. This suggests that the memory is not totally lost, but for some reason it is very hard to recall.

Are dreams in color?

3 Most dreams are in color. However, people may not be aware of it, either because they have difficulty remembering their dreams or because color is such a natural part of visual experience. People who are very aware of color while awake probably notice color more often in their dreams.

Do dreams have meaning?

4 Although scientists continue to debate this issue, most people who work with their dreams, either by themselves or with others, find the interpretation very meaningful. Dreams can help dreamers learn more about their feelings, thoughts, behavior, motives, and values. Many people find that dreams can help them solve problems. Furthermore, artists, writers, and scientists often get creative ideas from dreams.

How can I learn to interpret my dreams?

5 The most important thing to keep in mind is that your dreams reflect your underlying thoughts and feelings; the people, actions, settings, and emotions in your dreams are personal to you. Some dream experts believe that certain dreams and dream elements may be typical across different persons, cultures, and times. Usually, however, the same image will have different meanings for different people. For example, an elephant in a dream may mean one thing to a zookeeper and something quite different to a child whose favorite toy is a stuffed elephant. To learn to understand your dreams, think about what each dream element means to you or reminds you of. Then look for parallels between your dreams and what is happening in your waking life, and be patient and persistent.

Adapted from *www.asdreams.org*.

Before you read

Using previous knowledge

How much do you know about dreams? Answer these questions.

1. Do dreams have meaning? _____

2. Are dreams in color? _____

3. Does everyone dream? _____

4. How can I learn to interpret my dreams? _____

5. Why do people have trouble remembering their dreams? _____

_____

Reading

Scanning

Scan the text to check your answers. Then read the whole text.

After you read

Understanding details

A **Circle the answer that is *not* true.**

1. What do we know about REM sleep?
   a. It happens more than once a night.
   b. It is during REM sleep that people experience all their dreams.
   c. Except for the final REM period, REM sleep usually lasts less than 45 minutes.
2. How can remembering dreams be helpful?
   a. The dreamer may be able to understand his or her feelings better.
   b. The dreamer may get useful ideas in his or dream.
   c. The dreamer may be able to predict the future.
3. What do we know about the meaning of dreams?
   a. A dream about snow means something different to a Canadian and a Mexican.
   b. A dream about a car will mean the same thing to you and a friend.
   c. There are connections between your dreams and your waking life.

Understanding complex sentences

B **Separate each sentence from the text into two or three new sentences.**

1. (par. 2) By morning, people forget *nearly everything that happens throughout the night.*
   Dreams, thoughts that occur, and memories of brief awakening happen at night.

2. (par. 3) However, people may not be aware of it. This may be because _____
   _____. This may be because _____
   _____.

3. (par. 4) Scientists continue _____. There are people who
   work _____. These people find _____
   _____.

Relating reading to personal experience

C **Answer these questions.**

1. What do you think a dream about an elephant means to a zookeeper? What does it mean to a child whose favorite toy is a stuffed elephant?
2. Has a dream ever helped you solve a problem? If so, what was it?
3. Have you ever gotten a creative idea from a dream? If so, what was it?

What is a dream?

Some people think that when you dream, your mind is trying to tell you something. Other people, however, downplay the significance of dreams.

1 For centuries, people have wondered about the strange places that they seem to visit in their sleep. They have been dismissed as nonsense wanderings of the mind, meaningless nighttime journeys. However, they have been equally valued as necessary to a person's emotional and physical well-being.

2 Historically, people thought dreams contained messages from God. It was only in the twentieth century that people started to study dreams scientifically, believing that they reveal something about a person's character.

3 First, there was Sigmund Freud's wish-fulfillment theory. Freud was probably the first person to study dreams scientifically. In his famous book, *The Interpretation of Dreams,* in 1900, he wrote that dreams allow a person to express fantasies and fears, which would be socially unacceptable in real life.

4 The second theory to become popular was Carl Jung's compensation theory. Jung, a former student of Freud, said that the purpose of a dream is not to hide something, but rather to communicate it to the dreamer. He thought people should try to learn from their dreams. According to Jung, dreams make up for what is lacking in waking life. Thus, people who think too highly of themselves may dream about falling; those who think too little of themselves dream of being heroes.

5 Using more recent research, psychologist William Domhoff from the University of California, Santa Cruz, argues that dreams are not just a stage of sleep. They are connected to a person's waking hours, thoughts, and behavior. Among other things, Domhoff found that there is a connection between dreams and age, gender, and culture.

6 Dreaming is a mental skill that needs time to develop in humans. Children do not dream as much as adults. Until they reach age five, they cannot express very well what their dreams are about. Once people become adults, there is little or no change in their dream content.

7 The dreams of men and women differ. For instance, the characters that appear in the dreams of men are often other men, and often involve physical aggression. Domhoff found this same feature in the dreams of people from 11 societies. However, he also noted differences in their dreams. For instance, animals often show up in the dreams of people from traditional societies.

8 The meaning of dreams continues to be difficult to understand. However, those who study them agree that people should not take their dreams as reality. If you dream that a loved one is going to die, do not panic. The dream may have meaning, but it does not mean that your loved one is going to die.

Adapted from *The Sunday Times.*

Before you read

Look at the phrases below. Find out the meanings of any words you don't know. Then check (✔) those you think you will read in the text.

_____ 1. *the significance of dreams*   _____ 5. *discussions on television*
_____ 2. *emotional and physical well-being* _____ 6. *study dreams scientifically*
_____ 3. *wake up in the middle of the night* _____ 7. *express fantasies and fears*
_____ 4. *messages from God*   _____ 8. *connected to a person's waking hours*

Reading

Scan the text to check your predictions. Then read the whole text.

After you read

A **What do these words refer to? Circle the correct answer.**

1. *they* (par. 1, line 3)   ⓐ people   b. strange places
2. *They* (par. 1, line 4)   a. people   b. dreams
3. *they* (par. 1, line 8)   a. people   b. dreams
4. *it* (par. 4, line 7)   a. the purpose   b. something
5. *this same feature* (par. 7, lines 6, 7)   a. physical aggression   b. dreams of men
6. *their* (par. 7, line 10)   a. traditional ones   b. people from 11 societies

B **Check (✔) the correct column.**

	Inference	Restatement	Not in the text
1. Not everyone agrees that dreams are meaningful.		✓	
2. Writers of the 18th and 19th centuries wrote about the subject of dreams.			
3. There were scientific studies of dreams in the 19th century.			
4. According to Freud, people dream about things that they cannot talk about.			
5. Jung believed that people should think a lot about their dreams.			
6. Things that happen to you during the day can affect your dreams at night.			
7. Teenagers dream as much as adults.			
8. People in different societies dream about different things.			

C **Answer these questions.**

1. What do you often dream about? Why do you think you have these dreams?
2. Would you like to learn to interpret your dreams? Why or why not?
3. Which of the following things do you dream about most often: animals, water, nature, flying, friends, relatives, religion, sports, money, school, or work?

Vocabulary expansion

A **Write the letter of the correct definition next to each sleep-related phrase.**

_e_ 1. *doze off*
_____ 2. *drift off*
_____ 3. *hit the sack*
_____ 4. *go out like a light*
_____ 5. *grab some sleep*

_____ 6. *sleep in*
_____ 7. *sleep like a log*
_____ 8. *sleep through*
_____ 9. *toss and turn*

a. sleep very well
b. stay asleep while something noisy is happening around you
c. go to bed
d. fall asleep gradually
e. fall asleep when you do not intend to
f. sleep until you are ready to wake up
g. stop what you are doing in order to sleep for a short time
h. change your position in bed because you are unable to sleep
i. fall asleep immediately

B **Complete each sentence using one of the phrases from exercise A.**

1. I was starting to _____*doze off*_____ when the telephone rang.

2. I'll go home and _____ before we have to leave for the train station.

3. His mother reads him bedtime stories until he starts to _____.

4. Despite the all the activity, I somehow managed to _____ the earthquake!

5. She had to _____ for a few hours before falling asleep because the bed was very uncomfortable.

6. I'm so exhausted that I will probably _____ as soon as my head hits the pillow.

7. I don't like to get up early. I can't wait until the weekend because I can finally _____.

8. It's been a long day. I'm going upstairs to _____. Good night!

Sleep and you

What advice can you give to people who have trouble sleeping at night? Make a poster called "Trouble sleeping? Try these ten tips."

Acknowledgments

Illustration credits

Matt Collins	**5, 30, 39, 112**
Adam Hurwitz	**38, 60, 120**
Tim Rickard	**78, 98, 110, 126**
Daniel Vasconcellos	**42, 53, 82, 108, 118, 122**
William Waitzman	**2, 22, 41** (bottom), **44, 48, 59, 62, 72, 86, 94, 116**

Photographic credits

4 Bettmann/Corbis

6 John Kelly/The Image Bank/Getty Images

8 (*left to right*) Corbis; Reuters NewMedia Inc./Corbis

10 Getty Images

12 Andy Sacks/Stone/Getty Images

14 Reuters NewMedia Inc./Corbis

18 Getty Images

20 (*top to bottom*) Ron Chapple/Getty Images; Ron Lewine/Corbis

26 Duomo/Corbis

28 (*left to right, top to bottom*) Getty Images; Joe McBride/Stone/Getty Images

34 (*left to right, top to bottom*) Graham Neden/Ecoscene/Corbis; Bettmann/Corbis; James A. Sugar/Corbis

36 Getty Images

46 (*left to right, top to bottom*) Wayne Eastep/Stone/Getty Images; Owen Franken/Corbis; Pauline Cutler/Stone/Getty Images

50 Stewart Cohen/Stone/Getty Images

52 Getty Images

54 Sean Murphy/Stone/Getty Images

66 (*top to bottom*) Pam Gardner, Frank Lane Picture Agency/Corbis; Getty Images

68 Raymond Gehman/Corbis

70 Douglas Peebles/Corbis

75 (*left to right*) Jeff Hunter/The Image Bank/Getty Images; Patrick Ward/Corbis; Karen Huntt Mason/Corbis; Roman Soumar/Corbis

76 Buddy Mays/Corbis

80 (*left to right*) Foto World/Getty Images; Tim Barnett/Taxi/Getty Images; PhotoSpin; Steve Mason/Getty Images

84 Getty Images

90 Darama/Corbis

92 Tom Stewart/Corbis

100 Corbis

102 Courtesy of The Sharper Image

106 David Turnley/Corbis

114 James Darell/Getty Images

124 Lester Lefkowitz/Corbis

Text credits

The authors and publishers are grateful for permission to reprint the following items:

2 Adapted from "Lift Your Spirits with Music," *Woman's Day*, August, 2000, volume 63, Issue 13, page 13. Reprinted with permission from WOMAN'S DAY magazine. Copyright © 2000 by Hachette Filipacchi Media U.S., Inc.

4 From MARSALIS ON MUSIC by Wynton Marsalis. Copyright © 1995 by Wynton Marsalis and Sony Classical USA. Used by permission of W.W. Norton & Company, Inc.

6 Adapted from "The biology of music," *The Economist*, February 12, 2000, U.S. Edition, © 2000 The Economist Newspaper Group, Inc. Reprinted with permission. Further reproduction prohibited. www.economist.com.

10 Adapted from "It's not what you earn, it's what you keep," by Janet Bigham Bernstel, *Bank Rate Monitor*, 1997. Copyright © 1997 Bank Rate Monitor. All rights reserved. http://aol.thewhiz.com/brm/

12 Adapted from "Cheap Thrills," by Jill Jordan Sieder, *People Weekly*, May 5, 1997, volume 47, number 17, page 141.

14 Adapted from "Not a Lotto Luck: Pity the poor jackpot winners," by Lois Gould, *The New York Times Magazine*, May 1995. Copyright © 1995 by the New York Times Co. Reprinted by permission.

18 Adapted from "Your First Job," *Glamour*, September 1994, page 152. Copyright © 1994 Conde Nast Publications.

20 Adapted from "Different folks have varied reasons for why they like their jobs," by Joan Lloyd, *Milwaukee Journal Sentinel*, June 11, 2000, Employment Section page 01Z. Copyright Joan Lloyd, Joan Lloyd and Associates, management consulting firm (www.JoanLloyd.com)

22 Adapted from "Proud of working late? You may be compulsive," by Carrie Ferguson, *The Nashville Tennessean*, February 25, 2000, page E6. Copyright © 2000 The Tennessean.

26 Adapted from "Show me the money! Do pro athletes make too much money?" CURRENT EVENTS® May 5, 1997, Vol. 96, Issue 26. Reprinted by special permission from Weekly Reader Corporation. CURRENT EVENTS® is published by Weekly Reader. All rights reserved.

28 This article first appeared in *The Christian Science Monitor* on November 5, 1999, and is reproduced with permission. © 1999 The Christian Science Monitor (www.csmonitor.com). All rights reserved.

30 Adapted from the website http://www.perseus.tufts.edu/Olympics/sports.html. This material is used by permission of the Perseus Project at Tufts University (http://www.perseus.tufts.edu).

34 Adapted from "Keeping an Eye on the Weather," *Kids Discover*, December 1992, pages 12-13.

36 The book *Nature's Weather Forecasters* is written and illustrated by Helen R. Sattler, and published by Thomas Nelson Inc™ Copyright © 1978. Used by permission.

38 Adapted from "The Disaster-Ready Home," *McCall's Magazine*, May 1993, pages 100-106.

42 Adapted from "The interviewer may be wearing Birkenstocks, but some things never change," by Candee Wilde, *Computerworld*, April 1, 1998, page 62. Copyright (1998) COMPUTERWORLD, Inc. Reprinted with permission of Computerworld Magazine.

44 Adapted from "Casual Dress in the Workplace: A Controversial Trend," by Kathleen Driscoll, *Gannett News Service*, December 16, 1994.

46 Adapted from "One for all: Philadelphia tries on school uniforms," *The Columbus Dispatch*, Editorial and Comment, May 13, 2000, page 10A. REPRINTED, WITH PERMISSION, FROM THE COLUMBUS DISPATCH.

50 Adapted from "Adventures in India: Scribbled Travel Notes" from the website http://www.climbtothestars.org/india/ © **Stephanie Booth** aka Tara Star (**tara@climbtothestars.org**) created November 2000.

52 Adapted from GESTURES: THE DO'S AND TABOOS OF BODY LANGUAGE AROUND THE WORLD, by Roger E. Axtell. Copyright © 1991. This material is used by permission of John Wiley & Sons, Inc.

54 Adapted from "Managing Organisations in a Changing Multicultural Environment," by Neil Kendrick, *The Organisation*, Vol. 2, Issue 1, April-June 1999.

58 From *Living in Space* by Don Berliner. Copyright 1993 by Lerner Publications, a division of Lerner Publishing Group. Used by permission of the publisher. All rights reserved.

60 PP. 312-14 from DON'T KNOW MUCH ABOUT GEOGRAPHY by Kenneth C. Davis. Copyright © 1992 by Kenneth C. Davis. Reprinted by permission of HarperCollins Publishers Inc. WILLIAM MORROW/AVON BOOKS COPUB. Kenneth C. Davis is the author of the DON'T KNOW MUCH ABOUT® series, which includes DON'T KNOW MUCH ABOUT® HISTORY, DON'T KNOW MUCH ABOUT® GEOGRAPHY, DON'T KNOW MUCH ABOUT® THE CIVIL WAR, DON'T KNOW MUCH ABOUT® THE BIBLE, and DON'T KNOW MUCH ABOUT® THE UNIVERSE. Davis is also the author of DON'T KNOW MUCH ABOUT® children's books. Visit Kenneth C. Davis at his website, www.DontKnowMuch.com.

62 Adapted from "Unearthly Getaways; Space Tours Not So Far Off," by Michael Clancy, *The Arizona Republic*, May 4, 2000, page E1.

66 Used with permission from DID YOU KNOW?: New Insights into a World That Is Full of Astonishing Facts and Astounding Stories. Copyright © 1993 by The Reader's Digest Association, Inc., Pleasantville, New York, www.rd.com.

68 Adapted from "New York's Wild Kingdom: Lions and Tigers and Bears, oh my – all have been found in somebody's city apartment," *Newsday*, June 25, 1994, page C2.

70 Adapted from "For the animal's sake, let's abandon zoos," by Susan A. Scholterer, *The Buffalo News*, April 4, 2000, editorial page 2B.

74 The Big Book of Adventure Travel © James C. Simmons, Published by Avalon Travel Publishing.

76 Adapted from "Choosing an Ecodestination," Courtesy The International Ecotourism Society. www.ecotourism.org.

78 Adapted from *Overcoming Jet Lag* by Charles F. Ehret and Lynne Walker Scanlon, pages 16-18. Copyright © 1983 Berkley Books (200 Madison Ave. New York, New York 10016).

82 Adapted from "Star-crossed Asian lovers click with Net matchmaker," by Stephen Farrell, *The Times* (London), March 30, 2000, Copyright © 2000. Times Newspapers Limited.

84 Excerpted from "Cry for Help on the Internet" by Malcolm McConnell. Reprinted with permission from *Reader's Digest*, October 1997. Copyright © 1997 by The Reader's Digest Assn., Inc.

86 Adapted from "Count me out," *The Statesman* (India), May 29, 2000, Copyright © 2000 The Statesman Ltd. Reprinted by permission of the author.

90 Adapted from "10 easy ways to make friends," by Alison Bell, *'TEEN*, April 1994, pages 48, 49, and 94.

92 From BEST FRIENDS by Sharon J. Wohlmuth and Carol Saline, Copyright © 1998 by Carol Saline, Photographs © by Sharon J. Wohlmuth. Used by permission of Doubleday, a division of Random House, Inc.

94 "The New Family." Adapted extracts from an article by Vanessa Thorpe first published in *The Independent*, February 26, 1998, page 16.

98 From *A Celebration of Customs and Rituals* by Robert Ingpen and Philip Wilkinson. Copyright © Dragon's World Ltd, 1996, 1994. Copyright © Text Philip Wilkinson, 1996, 1994. Reprinted by permission of Facts on File, Inc.

100 Adapted from "Modern Day 'Gift of the Magi,'" *Dr. Laura on Radio*, December 1, 2000, Copyright © 2001 Premiere Radio Networks – all rights reserved. http://www.drlaura.com/letters/

102 Adapted from *The New Millennium 2001 Sharper Image Catalog*, pages 4, 13, and 69.

106 Adapted from "Jokes Can't Always Make You Laugh." Steve Wilson is a psychologist and founder and Cheerman of The Bored of the World Laughter Tour, whose mission is leading the world to health, happiness and peace through laughter and the formation of laughter clubs. He is the author of "Laugh 'Till It Helps!" For more information go to www.LaughterClubs.com <http:www.LaughterClubs.com> or call 1-800-669-5233 (U.S. & Canada).

108 Adapted from "Envy: is it hurting or (surprise) helping you?" by Julie Taylor, *Cosmopolitan*, March 3, 1998, Vol. 224, page 158.

110 Adapted from "Cheers for Tears," by Trudy Culross. This article originally appeared in *Redbook*, October 1994, page G-6.

114 Adapted from *The Cook's Encyclopedia of Chocolate*, by Christine McFadden and Christine France, pages 39 and 57. Barnes and Noble Books. Copyright © 2000.

116 Adapted from "The bitter truth about Popeye's Spinach," by Adam Sage, *The Times* (London), November 11, 2000. Copyright © 2000 Times Newspapers Limited.

118 Adapted from GESTURES: THE DO'S AND TABOOS OF BODY LANGUAGE AROUND THE WORLD, by Roger E. Axtell. Copyright © 1991. This material is used by permission of John Wiley & Sons, Inc.

122 Adapted from "Power Napping is Good for the IQ," *The Scotsman*, June 6, 2000. Copyright © 2000 The Scotsman Publications Ltd.

124 Adapted from © Association for the Study of Dreams, www.asdreams.org

126 Adapted from "Can it be a wake-up call?" by Lea Wee, *The Sunday Times* (Singapore), May 30, 1999, Sunday Plus Health Section, page 5. Copyright © 1999 The Straits Times Press Limited. Reprinted by permission of *The Sunday Times*.

Every effort has been made to trace the owners of copyright material in this book. We would be grateful to hear from anyone who recognizes their copyright material and who is unacknowledged. We will be pleased to make the necessary corrections in future editions of the book.